Yes, I'm in Love with Lawn Bowling

On-Kow Au

First Printing 2005

Produced by W & Y Cultural Products Co.
P.O. Box 44112, 6508 E. Hastings St. Burnaby, B. C.
V5B4Y2 Canada
Cover design by Paul Lee

Second Printing 2017

Printed in the United States Of America
CreateSpace Independent Publishing Platform

Yes, I'm in Love with Lawn Bowling is available in soft cover at Amazon websites worldwide, major online retailers and bookstores including CreateSpace, Barnes & Noble (USA), Bowker Books, Books A Million, Book Depository, Indie Bound, Alibris, Angus & Robertson (Australia), Bookworld (Australia), Wordery, Powells and libraries and academic institutions worldwide through the Ingram Content Group and Baker & Taylor, as well as NACSCORP in the USA.

Acknowledgements

I am grateful to the following organizations and persons for their generous sponsorship of the production and printing cost of this book:

Bowls B. C.

Janet Fung
(Stanley Park LBC, BC, Canada)
(Kowloon Cricket Club, Hong Kong)

Josephine Lee
(New Westminster LBC, BC, Canada)
(Granville Park LBC, BC, Canada)

Freeman Watt
(New Westminster LBC, BC, Canada)

Kion Wong
(Richmond LBC, BC, Canada)

And the support of an anonymous sponsor.

I also wish to thank Sophia Li and Tao Zhang for providing the cover photograph, and the following people for their assistance: Geoffrey Pershick, Steve Santana, Ricki Chan and Belle Chan.

Last but not least, I would like to thank Fong Ying Yu for his help in proofreading the draft.

Contents

Introduction to Lawn Bowls
Foreword
A Letter from David Bryant
Preface

Introduction to Lawn Bowls

Evidence exists of the ancient Egyptians playing a form of bowls over 7,000 years ago, when the object of the game was to "hit" the target. In the 13th century the game was first recorded as one of delicate skill, the object being to get the bowl as close as possible to the target.

Progress of the game in England had some interesting moments in history. Intent on the bowmen of England having their archery practice, Edward III banned the playing of bowls in the early 14th century, yet it still remained very popular. Later, King Henry passed an act forbidding any but the wealthy from playing the game. The act was not repealed until 1845, and once it was repealed, the game began to flourish in Great Britain.

Today, a favoured leisure pursuit of people the world over, bowls has taken its place as one of the popular sports of our time. The game is now played in 35 countries all over the world.

In Canada, lawn bowls is played socially and competitively in clubs from coast to coast. There are over 250 clubs in Canada with membership close to 17,000. In the Province of British Columbia alone, there are 54 clubs, mostly located next to public parks, with membership around 4,800.

The Association, "Bowls B.C.", supports bowling for all ages and encourages young and old to participate in this sport of a lifetime.

LAWN BOWLS IS

A game of skill and strategy
Challenging & rewarding
A community based sport
A mixed activity for both genders
For all ages
Easy to learn
Very sociable
Family oriented
Affordable
Accessible
Adaptable
Bowls Canada Boulingrin

Foreword

To many people, Lawn Bowling is a simple, straight forward pastime. To the great David J. Bryant, it is a Science, an Art Form, and the subject of a lifetime.

The lessons of lawn bowling and life itself have much in common and can be favourably compared.

We get out of it what we put into it.

This book contains a wealth of technical advice, useful hints, and a good helping of humour. It is highly readable and most enjoyable.

YES, I'M IN LOVE WITH LAWN BOWLING has rewarded me with a host of pleasant memories.

Well done On-Kow and thanks.
Graham W. Jarvis

A letter from David Bryant

Dear On-Kow,

I was delighted to receive your book and found the content most interesting and amusing. Thank you for thinking of me. Regretably, the decline in bowls is world wide and unfortunately England is no exception. There is however a growth in the number of youngsters taking up the game which is particularly good for the sport and very encouraging for the associations. At top level the game is flourishing but at club level numbers are dropping and many clubs are struggling to survive.

Reading your book reminded me of the many friends I made during my international days. Most of whom, like myself, are no longer competing at the very top. It is however nice to hear they are still involved in the game and passing on their expertise to others.

Bowls like most sports is very competitive at all levels but to me it is very special in that there is a camaraderie which exists throughout the world which I feel is unique and reading your book illustrates this. It is very obvious to the reader the enjoyment you have received in playing the game at both club and international level and your boundless enthusiasm for bowls comes shining through.

I am sure your book will become a collectors item as it is different from other books. Your love and dedication for the game are very apparent to the reader and it is obvious you have a delightful sense of humour which I believe is very important in bowls. A four who enjoy playing together with a positive attitude invariably do well.

Thank you once again for your delightful gift.

Yours sincerely,
David J. Bryant,
5th July 2005

Preface

I can never write like David Bryant or Tony Allcock. And yet, I can be a collector - gather the experiences, insights and wisdom of men and women bowlers who care enormously about sharing with others what they have learnt.

This book is specially written for people who discover the joy of being a bowler. By reading the stories of other people, you know you are not alone. By learning from those top champion bowlers, you can become a better bowler yourself.

On the green, there might be sweat and tears. However, there is always the lighter side of everything.

Hope that you enjoy reading this book and that my drawings brighten your day.

On-Kow Au
December, 2004

Chapter 1

The Sport of a Life Time

Ω

My Story

I T ALL STARTED in the air – I mean literally, up in the sky. It was the summer of 1998 when I was in the airplane. I was flying home from the National Team Training Camp in Kitchener, Ontario. Christine Soukoroff was sitting next to me. Both of us were excited - we both had something to look forward to. I would be sent to play in the Commonwealth Games and she in the North America Challenge. This had been an enjoyable week of training with well-organized program by head coach Bill Boettger and enlightening talks by the sports psychologist, Dave Scott, who perked up the spirits of all participants.

I was especially fortunate to have Elizabeth Templin, a lady with a heart of gold, as my billet. She treated me with great hospitality. Moreover, Truitjew Wagner, a member of the Heritage Greens LBC, took care of me like a mother by preparing Chinese food for my lunch and showing me around sightseeing. Most impressive of all was the chance to meet so many devoted bowlers. Throughout the week, the only topic of conversation was lawn bowling. We talked about it practically all the time. I remember on one occasion that Christine, me, Truitjew and her friend, who was not a bowler, were having lunch together in a restaurant. The three of us couldn't help talking about lawn bowling through the whole meal, leaving that poor woman out by herself, And even when the Camp was over, Christine and I were still talking about it on our return journey. What kind of people are we who are so crazy about a game of throwing round balls? In the plane, we were so involved with our thoughts that we ventured to discuss the possibility of writing a book on lawn bowling.

"Y-Y-E-E-S-S," came straight out of my mouth, "I'm in love with lawn bowling. This will be the title of the book".

When we were home, we went back to our normal lives. We did mention the idea of writing a book to a few bowlers. Then the whole thing died down. I knew that not one soul took us seriously. Everyone, including myself, just thought it was a beautiful dream, a dream that would never come true.

Four years passed. In 2002, the Canadian Junior Championship was held in Victoria, B.C. Reading the results from "The Green," I saw the name Andrew Wagner, who won the "under 16" title. That name rang a bell. The article interviewed Andrew's mother Truitjew. Oh, yes, Andrew is Truitjew's son. Immediately, an image of some young kids flashed back in my mind. I remember in the Camp four years ago, when we were having a BBQ at the club house one evening, I saw several young kids aged about 10 to 12 were having a game on the green. It was a delightful sight to watch them happily jumping up and down the green, enjoying the game. Truitjew told me they were her son Andrew and his cousins from the States who came to stay for the summer vacation. Judging from the way they played, you couldn't believe that they were brand new bowlers.

I wrote a letter to Truitjew, congratulating her on her son's success. Immediately, I received a long letter from Truitjew, telling me every detail of her trip to Victoria and how she spent sleepless nights before the game and how happy she was that Andrew won the gold medal. I could feel the joy and enthusiasm reading the letter. We haven't changed a bit. Our passion for the sport remains the same.

In these few years, many things happened. Some good bowlers disappeared from the scene, and yet lots of new bowlers have come up. I have retired from my work and have more free time. Maybe it is time to pursue what I wanted to do four years ago. I started thinking about it for some time. Finally, I decided to launch the project ahead no matter how difficult it looked. I still have the passion which motivates me to make this dream come true.

I always feel sorry to see that lawn bowling is not a popular sport here. Some people say that they will give lawn bowling a try only after they have retired. Life is short and they don't know how much they are missing in their procrastination. It is not surprising to hear those people who really start bowling after retirement say the same thing: they wish they would have started ten years earlier.

Every bowler has a story to tell as to how they started. I started bowling in my forties. At that time, my husband C.P. and I were busy with our work of radio program productions in Hong Kong. To release the tension, we joined a private club, the Craigengower Cricket Club for its recreational facilities such as badminton and tennis courts and swimming pool. One day, when we walked past the bowling green to the parking lot, a club member called John Pau grabbed our arms and pulled us to the green. He showed us a bowl and insisted that we should try it. We knew nothing about lawn bowling then. But out of curiosity, we tried to throw it. Funnily enough, both of us found it a very interesting sport. Soon we joined the club team and played in the leagues, and later in competitions. In no time, we got hooked.

To be honest, I never enjoy any other sports like I do lawn bowling. I always feel happy when I step on the green. When the bowl slips out of my hand, it might be light or heavy, wide or narrow, yet I have fun rolling it again and again till I finally get the skill right. It is an unspeakable joy to see how the bowl stops where I want it to, hits the right bowl or trails the jack. In the game situation, there's always fun, satisfaction and a sense of achievement when I play well and apply the right strategy. Yes, I'm in love with lawn bowling. I always feel grateful to old John who introduced me to such a great sport which lasts a life time. This sport is truly amazing and offers each of us something special.

Actually, lawn bowling is more than a sport to me. Two years later, in 1989, when I emigrated to Canada, lawn bowling helped me to adjust my life quickly to the mainstream. Through lawn bowling, I got to know a lot of friends, and visited different places. When I became a member of the Canadian National Team from 1995 to 2000, I had the opportunity to go to cities I never dreamt that I would have the chance to visit. And I know I would never feel lonely even when I grow old if I can still be a bowler.

Start Young

Because a bowler can bowl to an old age, lawn bowling may give people the impression of an old person's game. You can bowl when you get older, but you don't have to be older to enjoy it. Actually, many people start young. One of the top bowlers in Canada, the late Edwin (Ted) Waterston, was one of them. Many years ago, when I first knew him, I was fascinated by his superb skills in bowling. I asked him how many years he had been bowling. "Forty years," he answered. With wide open eyes, I asked how old he was. "Forty-seven," he said. Yes, he started bowling when he was seven in Scotland and played it ever since. In his own words, he ate in order to live and he lived in order to bowl. Life would be meaningless to him without lawn bowling. I often wonder what turned this born rebel, genuine hippie, nonconformist into a lawn bowl fanatic. But with regret, I can never get an answer from him now. May God rest his soul.

Many world champion bowlers in fact started their bowling careers at very young ages. For example: Tony Allcock at l2, David Bryant at 9, John Bell at 13, Willie Wood at 12. David Bryant's maxim is, "Bowls is a young man's game that old men can play."

Dave Brown, the Canadian National Team coach, started bowling when he was six in England. His father and grandfather were good bowlers. He still can remember when he was seven, his dad handmade a set of wooden bowls the size a little larger than a jack and put them in his Christmas stockings. But it was when he attended boarding school, which always encouraged students to play all sports, that he generated an interest in competitive sports. At the age of twelve, he ventured road racing cycling and when he grew older, he even went to professional soccer for two years. Then he was conscripted. After serving in the army, he devoted most of his free time to lawn bowling and kept winning in competitions. A long-time member of the Canadian National Team, he secured two gold medals, two silver medals and two bronze medals in international games.

A lot of good bowlers who come from Britain are of similar background. Graham Jarvis, another top bowler and my mentor in bowling, also started bowling when he was six in Scotland. He remembered there was a sports complex near the place he lived, which was also the main lawn bowling centre. When his grandfather and father bowled there, he and his brother would make use of the adjacent empty space next to the bowling green. They put the jack between the trees and threw bowls and had lots of fun. Most of the time, he watched his father play and learnt.

The most exciting thing was real participation in the game. When his father played singles in the club in the evenings, he would sit on the bench lining up with other boys waiting to be called as markers. His happiest moment was to carry bowls for his dad, and his dad would ask the opponent, "Do you mind if my son marks for us?" Usually the opponent had no objection. Then he, just a little boy of six or seven, would do what a proper marker should do by setting the jack, keeping the scoreboard, answering questions and sometimes even doing the measuring. And after the game, he got paid three pennies from each player.

He and his brother Tom became very good bowlers and often bowled together. They came to Canada in 1957. And one year later, in 1958, they won practically every game there was to win in Vancouver. All these years, he won a total of 15 BC gold medals and 5 National gold medals. He has been in the National Team since 1974 and won a silver medal in the l980 World Bowls.

In England

Beryl Harrington, a many-time Canadian gold medalist who came to Canada in the early 90's, gave us more information about lawn bowling in England.

In England, everyone has somebody in the family who is a bowler. Every park has a bowling green. When she was small and went to the park, there were two places which children were not allowed to enter. One was the cricket area and the other was the lawn bowling green. And yet every single child was exposed to lawn bowling. She can still remember when she was a young girl, she had to watch the TV programs her parents watched. There was a lawn bowling TV show hosted by David Bryant every Sunday night which was influential in increasing the popularity of the sport.

Every big company had a bowling green and the employees had to bowl for the company. The place Beryl lived in was only a small town and yet there were altogether 25 clubs. All through the summer, there were at least three competitive games a week. In Canada, we get used to mentioning there are social bowlers and competitive bowlers. But in England, there is no social bowling. All bowlers go into competitions, not for the money, but for the honour.

The incentive is to be a winner. The team is like a holy matrimony - "For better or for worse, till death do we part." The same team would stick together for life and seldom split. You have to form your own team in order to play. Going into competition was a learning process. In the major tournaments, entries would usually come up to over a thousand.

"Bowling is popular in England because it has always been there. It is part of the heritage." Beryl concluded.

In Canada

In Canada, a lot of good bowlers started young as well. The Canadian-born Alan Webster threw his first bowl when he was four. His father was the president of Terminal City LBC (now known as Granville Park LBC). He set up a family rule for his children that every year on the opening day of the club, only if they could throw four bowls to the ditch would they be allowed to join the club. Eventually, Alan made it when he was eleven. He was the youngest of four brothers, and only he turned out to be a good bowler. He remembered his first win was when he was 13 years old, he beat the 19-year-old Jim Morrison in the final and won the BC Week Novice Singles in 1968. Later, he stopped bowling for some years because of work and family. When everything had settled down, he became a serious bowler again in 1990. In 1998, he won the Provincial Singles and a silver medal in the National

Championship. In 1999, he won the BC Fours and a gold medal in the Nationals. His greatest achievement is to win a gold medal in the Singles for Canada in the 1999 Asia Pacific Games. Most families in Canada do not have such bowling heritage. John Aveline started bowling when he was sixteen. He grew up in a small town in Ontario. There was a bowling club across the street from where he lived. His neighbour invited him to try and he went there just out of curiosity. After receiving five minutes of coaching, he started bowling. In the first few years, he bowled purely socially in this small club with a membership of only twenty and knew nothing about competitive bowling. It was not until five years later that he learnt about the junior games and started to play singles in the district, and then teamed up with better bowlers. Later he moved to BC and bowled with high-caliber bowlers to win the Provincials and then the Nationals.

"I knew nothing about lawn bowling before I met John," John's wife Cathie said. "I was dating a world champion curler by that time. Then John came into my life and he taught me how to bowl. We enjoyed bowling together. Later I reached the Provincial level and had a chance to bowl in the North American Challenge. But no matter what my achievement was, there was no respect from my family and my friends for the sport. I like lawn bowling so much that I have the confidence to put up with all the negative feedback from people around me who are not bowlers."

Devoted to this sport as they are, both John and Cathie not only put a lot of time into bowling, they also hold various posts in the administration of the game. Their little toddler was literally brought up on the green from birth.

"I was still bowling when I was eight months pregnant. I remember it was a Friday league in the club, a bowler asked me what my due day was. I answered it was yesterday. I was sent to the labour ward that evening. I was also quick to go back to the green after giving birth. I remember when my daughter was three months old, I played in a game and breast-fed my baby in between the ends."

Do they expect their daughter to be a bowler one day?

"It is difficult to tell. We'll let her make her own choice when she grows up." John answered. "But she surely knows what bowling is even though she is only three years old. By watching what we do, she knows all the rules of the green. When she plays her small set of bowls, she would chalk the bowl if it hits the jack and she would ask me to stand behind her when she throws her bowls. Maybe by the time she grows up, there will be more appreciation for the game from the public which could encourage her to be a bowler. At least, she would get all the support from us."

Junior Program

Although some bowlers feel this game is not respected and is looked at as an old man's game, yet a Junior Program started to flourish in Victoria about ten years ago. It all started on a sunny afternoon when a couple of young boys, aged nine and thirteen, went to watch their oldest brother play baseball at the Burnside playground. Next to the field, they saw some people throwing round balls on the lawn. Out of curiosity, they peeked through the fence over the bowling green. Robin Forrest was, at that time, a member of Burnside Bowling Club. She invited them to come inside and Craig Wilson showed them how to throw bowls. Yes, the boys were the Kaufman brothers.

"When I first tried it, I thought it was just a fun game. Then I got a lot of encouragement from the club members. That year, I won the novice singles and then the South Island novice singles. I tasted the sweet joy of competitiveness. I practiced with a goal, hoping to win more games. A year after, when I was fourteen, I immediately played in the Provincial games. It was Craig who encouraged me to carry on being a good bowler. Now I have finished my studies and about to embark on my career and future. But I won't give up bowling. I have joined PBA and look forward to achieving something in this sport I love," Derek, the elder of the Kaufman brothers, said.

He and his brother Adam initiated a junior program in 1993. All through these years, it has succeeded in attracting a lot of youngsters to lawn bowling. Outstanding ones such as Steve Santana, Sherrey Sidel, Leanne Chinery and Heather Battles became so successful that they were not only winning the Junior Singles championship, but also gold medals in Provincials and Nationals, and went on to play in international games.

"I really enjoy coaching young people," Craig said in his bass voice, his eyes glittering, when I asked him about his experience in coaching the juniors.

"When you teach them and explain something, and they suddenly catch what you mean, you can see light coming out from their eyes. It's awesome. My strength is understanding kids. I don't indoctrinate them. I only give some advice after watching how they play. Kids don't like to be told to do this and that. Give them the free choice, and they learn to be independent. When you let them go their way, they'll develop their own wonderful style."

"It's awesome to watch them play. Young people have no fear. They don't think twice. They do those crazy things that you never expect to do, but they work."

Craig Wilson has been a field hockey coach since 1964. In those years, he coached the women's field hockey Provincial Team and University of Victoria women's team. Later, he decided to do coaching with young people, and he picked up lawn bowling. Craig's father was a champion bowler in New Zealand and Craig started bowling when he was sixteen.

"Lawn bowling is a very special sport," Craig said. "Whenever I step on the green, the world seems so far behind me and I have a feeling of peace and tranquility. I also love the level of skill. I think there is more skill required in it than any other sport."

Bowling Couples

Lawn bowling is a sport not only for people of different ages to enjoy, it is also a sport for the family, especially husband and wife. We may tease the wives of devoted bowlers as "lawn bowl widows" because their husbands often spend too much time on the green and not with them. But actually both husband and wife can be bowlers and enjoy the game as a couple.

Alice Duncalf, a many-time National gold medalist and former National Team member, became a bowler all because of husband Dave. Alice got to know Dave in 1970. Dave was in the National Team at that time, so Alice went to watch him play bowls through the whole summer. Then Dave started teaching her how to play. She tried it and liked it.

"Those women are blocking the road. Are they protesting?"
"Oh, yes, some people are on strike again.
What's new in Canada?"

Three weeks later, Dave proposed to her. Perhaps because his previous wife was not a bowler, they separated, amongst other reasons. He wanted to make sure that Alice liked lawn bowling and that she was the right one for him.

"We spent our honeymoon bowling together in the Pacific InterMountain Tournament in San Francisco. You can see how devoted we were. It is really wonderful that we shared the same interest," said Alice in reminiscence of the late Davie.

Another couple in the National Team is Keith and Jean Roney. Keith's parents were bowlers. But it was not until his father passed away in 1978, after which he had to drive his mother to the clubhouse, that he started to bowl himself. On the other hand, Jean was a golfer when she married Keith. Then Keith taught Jean how to bowl and in no time, both of them became very competitive bowlers. Keith likes a lot of other sports such as curling, soccer and hockey, but it was the unique challenge and competitiveness of the game that attracted him to lawn bowling. As a museum curator, Keith travels a lot to do research work. In all these years, both of them often travel together to bowl abroad and enjoy their bowling career very much.

Hong Kong Immigrants

Worldwide, bowls is played in countries with a historical connection to Great Britain. Hong Kong, being a former British Colony, retains a lot of British heritage such as lawn bowling. There, it has been looked upon as a sport for the elite. Only the colonial private sports clubs have bowling greens, and only the rich people with the necessary social status, or upper-class expatriates, belonged to these clubs.

"My minimal knowledge of lawn bowling was my memory of seeing some foreigners rolling bowls as I walked past the green when I was small," Freeman Watt, an immigrant from Hong Kong, said. "It's my father's old colleague Peter Ho who introduced me to the sport. Peter worked in the Hong Kong Telephone Company and learnt the game from a British co-worker. I always have an interest to be involved in the community. So, when I came to Vancouver in 1994, I joined the club here not only because of the sport, but also because of the social aspect. This is a friendly sport and I have the opportunities to meet new people and socialize. I participate in the club committee and also help to mow the green."

Both Freeman and his wife Josephine Lee bowl competitively, and both have won silver medals in the Provincial games. Josephine, a very promising bowler, won the women's singles in the 2004 Canadian Open tournament in Ontario.

"I started bowling after Freeman had bowled for four years," Josephine said. "At that time, I worked irregular hours and had no interest to try something I knew nothing about. The only thing I felt about lawn bowling was that Freeman was out all the time. That was until one night, he told me that he would be interviewed live in a radio program. I was on duty at the hospital that night. So I borrowed a transistor radio from my co-worker and listened to the program. It is funny that I had to get the message from my husband through the airwaves to arouse my interest for the sport. Then I joined New Westminster LBC in July. It was Marva Goddard who coached me. I bowled outdoor as well as indoor, and soon got hooked. I am a slow starter, but if I get determined to do something well, I will work hard on it. Usually I succeed."

It is interesting to see how a radio program triggered a chain reaction in the Chinese community to try lawn bowling six years ago. It all started when my husband and I picked up our old trade and worked in the local multicultural radio station.

The School Board was running some Chinese evening adult education programs and we became the instructors of a radio broadcasting course. The course manager was looking for any new and interesting subjects. Knowing that we were bowlers, she suggested running a new course to introduce lawn bowling. At that time, the Pacific Indoor LBC was very anxious to get more members, so we joined hands to start the venture. The program was quite successful with over fifty people attending. Quite a number of them joined indoor and then outdoor clubs. Later on, when we hosted an open-line radio show in the evening, we invited Ronnie Law and Freeman Watt to introduce lawn bowling to the public. The show made an impact. Many listeners started to try bowling and quite a number of them became devoted bowlers. A lot of them joined Richmond LBC because Richmond has a large Chinese community.

"We have nearly 300 members and over half are Chinese," Kion Wong, the newly elected president of the club, said.

Kion came to Canada in 1994, but it was not until 1997 that he joined the club through a friend. Both Kion and his wife Amy have talents for the sport and started playing well soon after. As third-year bowlers, they won the V&D Mixed Fours event in 2000. Pursuing championship success in the sport, however, is not their main interest. Both of them are happy just contributing their effort to the well-being of the club.

"I guess it's my personality. Even when I was small, I had a strong desire to do what I can for the community. In school, I was a boy scout and did volunteer work in the Red Cross," Kion explained.

"For the Richmond LBC, membership is never a problem for us. Every year we have a good turnout of new members. There was a year we had 80, and this year it is 40, which is good enough. We have enough people to replace the dropouts. My priority as the president is to improve the condition of the green and motivate more members to contribute to club activities. For competitive bowling, our bowlers have made themselves noticeable in lots of major tournaments. We even have junior bowlers who become very active with the support of their parents."

Like Kion, we have many bowlers who volunteer a lot of time and money for the sport. To them, I pay due respect. And I fully understand that there are times they feel discouraged when the onlookers criticize them for no reason. We may get some revelation from the following words of wisdom:

People are unreasonable, illogical, and self-centered.

Love them anyway.

If you do good, people may accuse you of selfish motives.

Do good anyway.

If you are successful, you may win false friends and true enemies.

Succeed anyway.

The good you do today may be forgotten tomorrow,

Do good anyway.

Honesty and transparency make you vulnerable,

Be honest and transparent anyway,

What you spend years building may be destroyed overnight.

Build anyway.

People who really want help may attack you if you help them.

Help then anyway.

Give the world the best you have and you may get hurt.

Give the world your best anyway.

The world is full of conflict.

Choose peace of mind anyway.

The Sport for All

Perhaps lawn bowling is one of the least physically demanding athletic activities. It is suitable for participants of both genders, all races, all ages, people with different body builds, or even people physically handicapped. All bowlers are born equal.

If you happen to walk by Vancouver's scenic Stanley Park LBC one day, you may see some social bowling in the afternoon draw. Then you may overhear on the green someone shouting, "Oh, this is a Peter Holt's shot." You must wonder if this is a new term in lawn bowling. A Peter Holt's shot means your bowl is two feet short. A joke with no hard feelings and well received with a laugh by the person himself. Yes, Peter Holt is a man without two legs and he is a bowler, a good bowler. He has a touching story to tell.

In July 1997, he came to Vancouver as a visitor. When he drove down Stanley Park along Beach Avenue, he saw the lawn bowling green which reminded him of Singapore where he worked in the 70's. He pulled over and went into the clubhouse with his wife. They were warmly welcomed and were invited to try to throw bowls. He tried and liked it. As an amputee for several years because of blood cancer, he considered the sport a great exercise and would serve as good physiotherapy. They paid the membership fees right way and joined the club. Later, on his second visit to the city, he spent more time on the bowling green and knew then this was definitely the sport for him. Among other things, lawn bowling was one of the reasons for his decision to move to Canada.

He had made the right decision. For, after he settled down in Vancouver and started playing well with only one leg, a devastating thing happened. He lost the other leg in 2000. With firm determination, the support of a great wife and the medical staff, he learned to walk, to drive and to bowl with two prosthetic legs.

"Bowling saved my sanity,"pondered Peter. "This sport keeps me going, not only the game, but the people. On the green, I get tremendous help from everybody. There's always someone picking up bowls or setting the jack for me. Such great comradeship changed me. Being a heavy equipment engineer and the supervisor in charge of the whole crew, I was a hardheaded person. Now I am a different person."

Yes, he is right. We all remember what he did for us during BC Week. We were so impressed to see how he walked around the green from time to time, holding a bottle of iced water to serve bowlers with drinks under the hot sunlight. We are thankful to know someone like Peter. His beaming face and cheerful voice teach us more about the courage to face catastrophe and the meaning of life.

Believe it or not, lawn bowling can work miracles. Janet Fung is a living example. In 1994, she went to England to attend her daughter's wedding. Unfortunately, she had a serious car accident on highway M11 which totally wrecked her upper body. Three of her ribs were broken, part of a lung was ruptured and the teeth, tongue and nose were crushed. She was sent back to Vancouver for treatment. It was a miracle that she survived. But for two years, she was so weak that she couldn't even lift up her body in the bed by herself. She was under medical treatment for five years. One day in 1999, she went for a stroll with her husband and daughter in Stanley Park. Suddenly, it started to rain heavily. They took shelter in the nearby building which happened to be the lawn bowling club. After chatting with the friendly club members, she was invited to try lawn bowling. Thinking it might help her health, she joined the coaching lessons. But after four sessions, she found her body couldn't cope and declined to continue. Fortunately, the kind-hearted coach Ann Maze persistently encouraged her. At last, with great effort, she attended the remaining sessions. Then something amazing happened. After the completion of the whole course, she had no difficulty with any body co-ordination and started to bowl.

"From that day onward, I recovered quickly. Whenever I step on the green, I forget all my pain and feel so happy. Now there's no need for me to take any medicine. I bowl nearly everyday. Usually in the winter, I go back to Hong Kong and bowl in the Kowloon Cricket Club. I even play in the Saturday League - B Division as lead or second. Lawn bowling is part of my life now."

Looking at the healthy, cheerful Janet, it is unbelievable that she had gone through such devastation.

Reading about the stories of so many bowlers, you must marvel at how great this game must be. Lawn bowling is well-described in the Bowls Encyclopedia:

"Bowls is a science, the study of a lifetime, in which you may exhaust yourself but not your subject. It is a contest, a dual calling for courage, skill and self-control. It is a test of temper, a trial of honour, a revealer of character. It affords the chance to play the man and act the gentleman.

It is a cure for care, an antidote of worry. It includes companionship with friends, sociability and the opportunity for courtesy, kindliness and generosity to an opponent. It provides not only physical health but also moral force."

Yes, this is a great game and truly a sport for life.

Chapter 2

Natural? Or Practice Makes Perfect?

Ω

Natural Ability

THERE IS TALENT in doing all things. What is the special knack that makes a champion bowler? When you ask a new bowler to throw the first bowl, some people can do it naturally and get the proper delivery right away. But some people have difficulty in even doing a simple action of throwing something out with the back swing of the arm. Dave Brown, who has been coaching lawn bowling to a lot of people, believes that some people have a natural ability in sports.

"By simply looking at how that person walks I can detect whether he is coachable or not," Dave said. "In lawn bowling, the talents are mainly the eyes and hand co-ordination, and of course the will to win. When you play bowls, you must have a relaxed body and, at the same time, mental sharpness towards the game. It works better when you start young because your body can adapt better. If you start late in life, your body might not work that well."

Alan Webster agrees that the talents in bowling are mainly the eyes and hand co-ordination, and also muscle memory - making the movement from proper combination of muscle actuation feel second nature. Your body movement must have the flexibility and you must have the ability to concentrate.

To become a champion bowler, Graham Jarvis reckons the following points applicable, in order of importance: athletic ability; good eyesight with accurate depth perception, in order to have an accurate plan view when one is on the mat; concentration; the desire to win; and fitness.

After the physical attributes, he considers concentration as perhaps the most important ingredient for success in bowls. He explains that concentration can be compared to burning a piece of paper with a magnifying glass. There is a certain focal point which would allow the sun's rays to heat the paper to flames. This is like the mental capacity of focusing and concentration. When you step on the mat and look at the jack, whether the jack is long or short, the green is quick or slow, your eyes should look at the object from which you start the mental process like a computer - sorting out all the information. It all starts from the eyes and all the way back to the mind. The mind is then able to signal the body for the appropriate weight control. After making sure that all information has been properly considered, if a bowler then believes he can execute the shot, chances are he will make the shot.

It seems, though, that Jarvis is too good at it. He once had an unforgettable experience during the 1980 World Bowls in Melbourne, Australia. He was skipping the Pairs team with Burnie Gill as the lead. Using his mental capacity to its fullest helped them achieve fifteen straight wins, but this was without realizing that he was nearly drained out. In the end, by winning 17 games out of 19, they won a silver medal. The Fours event followed the pairs but Jarvis collapsed after 14 games out of the 19 and required medical attention. It was the end of the Tournament for him and he was unable to attend the medal presentation. His full recovery required three weeks back home in Canada.

Athletic background

Cary Manns is a born athlete. Physically strong by being a firefighter, he has done well in four other sports. He played tennis at the tournament level. He is a Provincial champion and National silver medalist in hockey. He also played in the world and Canadian championships in lacrosse. Last but not least, he was also a good baseball player. His target is to add lawn bowling to the list as the fifth sport that he can play at the Provincial or National level.

"I can tell whether you are athletic by watching how you do it. The real athlete has a natural and rhythmic style in the delivery. Compared to other sports, lawn bowling has more finesse and great strategy."

When a person is good at other sports, it usually means he or she would pick up lawn bowling more easily than those who are not, especially of course if the other sport is similar to bowling.

Bill Boettger, one of the top bowlers in Canada, played 5-pin bowls before he tried lawn bowling. It was in 1963; he 5-pin bowled with then Canadian Pairs lawn bowling champions Ray Reidel and Joe Dorsch. At the bowling banquet, an invitation to the League was made to try lawn bowling as the season was just starting. About ten of them went out and ended up joining the club. George Boxwell was also one in this group.

"What attracted me to this sport is the variety," explained Bill. "There is the variety of games - singles, pairs, triples and fours. Also there is the variety of skills - from the touch of the draw to the powerful drives. Moreover, there is the variety of competitive levels from club games to international."

"I do consider myself a 'natural' as I have been intensely competitive in all things all my life, and the skill of bowls was an easy carry-over from my 5-pin alley bowling days, as far as the smooth delivery of different paced shots is concerned. I believe that I also have the mental strength to overcome adversity and to never give up."

Marlene Cleutinx, who is another one of the top bowlers in Canada and a former National Team member, played Belgium bowling before she turned to lawn bowling. Marlene belongs to the third generation of Belgium immigrants. Once, she won the Belgium Bowling Singles in Manitoba and went back to Belgium to compete. Long before bowling, she was also a curler in the 70's and curled at the Provincial level and played in the National Championship. She explained that the only common thing between curling and bowling is the hand and mind co-ordination. But for weight control, you use the whole body movement to send out the rock in curling, while in lawn bowling, you only use the arm. Also, the strategy of the two sports is different.

On the other hand, Jim Murphy, a champion bowler famous for having a natural and beautiful delivery, owes his ability in bowling to curling and softball. He believes there is a lot of similarity in the delivery between curling and bowling. As a softball pitcher, he has the same movement in the stepping forward of the foot and the swinging of the arm to throw the balls. It is natural for him to roll the bowl and he has no problems throwing a runner with ditch weight.

Mary Ann Gillies, a Provincial Singles gold medalist, was also a softball pitcher as well as a tennis player before she picked up lawn bowling. Laila Hassan, a National singles champion and former Hong Kong Team member, was yet another softball player when she was young. As a pitcher, she had all the strength that was required of her. And yet she turned to lawn bowling because she thinks softball is too physical. She wanted to have a sport that she can play for a lifetime. She was coached by the famous World Bowls gold medalist O.K. Dallah. Her softball background helps her to have the ability in delivering various shots.

"I have no problem playing on heavy greens and throwing runners. I remember once a male bowler said to me, "You drive like a man." I considered it a silly comment. My feedback to him was "Do you say to a man you draw like a woman?" "What attracts me to lawn bowling is the strategy of the game. It is a game of the mind and a lot of skill is involved."

All through our conversations, she stressed "the mind" a lot rather than the physical aspect of a bowler. Yes, it is true. Just as some people put it: The most important thing about lawn bowling is the "six inches." It is the distance between your two ears - your brain.

Mind Game

Dorothy Macey, a many-time National champion and a long-time National Team member, thinks along the same line. Both she and her husband Don have been involving in sports all of their lives as soccer and softball coaches at the community centre. Although Dorothy is a short lady of four feet eleven, she was active in track and field in school. Running was her specialty. And yet, when talking about the talents of a bowler, she said, "A top bowler must have intelligence which is in-born. Lawn bowling is like playing chess. It is about moves and counter-moves. You have to think ahead. Also, you need to be quick-minded. There are many times I can beat those higher skilled bowlers because I out-think them. Look at those top bowlers; they are all highly intelligent people."

Steve Forrest would also agree on the "mind game" of lawn bowling. Being outdoor and indoor National singles champion and a former National Team member, he also has a natural ability in sports. He said he got the genes from his grandfather who was also a champion bowler. When he was fourteen, he tried to play crown green bowling and mastered the skill after only two practices.

"A good bowler must have good concentration and be able to stay calm. There is similarity between bowling and golfing, although the physical skills are different. Mentally, both games are task oriented. You say to yourself - yes, I can do it, then you can really do it," said Steve, the golfer who has won a car once by hitting a hole-in-one.

Talents

"The ability to enjoy it is the talent." On a sunny day sitting on the balcony at North Vancouver LBC with me, Craig said this and pointed to the young people competing in the National Junior Canadian Championships on the green.

"Do you see that young boy, Stewart MacLean, from Prince Edward Island? Look at him. He is so relaxed and just throws the bowl out smoothly. You can see how he enjoys bowling. That is the talent."

Looking him up in the handbook, I found out that Stewart at only eleven years of age was the youngest competitor in this tournament. He has been bowling for three years and he also plays AAA hockey, Premiere Soccer, and is on the school's track and cross country teams.

Maybe this is a delightful yardstick to use to tell whether you have the talent for bowling. If you enjoy playing the game, you must have the talent for it. Don't we all enjoy playing the game and thus have the talent?

For a real genius like Ryan Bester, you not only see how he enjoys playing, but you enjoy watching him play. Ryan started bowling when he was ten. His uncle and grandfather are bowlers too. It was Ryan's two elder brothers who bowled first and then, two years later, Ryan started to bowl, followed by their father. The four of them bowled so well that they immediately won quite a number of medals in the Provincials.

Ryan has been a notch above the others to step on the ladder of success. By winning the WOBA, he got in the National Team and was sent to play in the Singles in the 2002 Commonwealth Games. That was when he was only seventeen.

"It was a wonderful experience for me. I bowled against the world's best singles players such as Tony Allcock and John Bell. I only lost two points to Mervyn King from England. I proved to myself that I could bowl at that caliber of competition. That gave me a lot of confidence," Ryan said.

It was his gold medal performance in World Bowl 2004 that shocked the bowling world. By teaming up with Keith Roney, who has been a National Team member for 18 years, they set Canadian lawn bowling history by winning the Pairs event. Added to this honour, this world championship neophyte was also voted as "Bowler of the Tournament."

I had a chance to watch Ryan's game when he played the Pairs with his father in the 2004 Canadian Championship, held in Vancouver. His drive shots were dynamite and he had a lot of skillful shots. Other than drawing, he played well in wicks and trails. His style of delivery reminds me of another bowling phenomenon, Bruce Matheson. Bruce is one of the best bowlers in Canada who came to the bowling scene about 30 years ago. He, too, started bowling as a teenager. In his early twenties, he won nearly every championship. Now, after Bruce, here comes Ryan.

"I never had a coach and I never asked anyone how to do things. Sometimes, I may talk to Bill Boettger, Ron and Kelvin Jones, and that's it. Everything comes to me naturally. How to take my line? I just look about 10 feet out. It's difficult to explain. And the weight control? I do it by feeling. And my drive shots? I go straight down, putting the feet and go accordingly. When to drive? Depending on the situation of the game. I do it all by instinct."

"What is your goal?"

"My goal is to be number one in the world," he immediately responded, eyes sparkling. Yes, the sky is the limit. We all wish him a very bright international career.

In BC, Hiren Bhartu has caught a lot of people's eyes in recent years by winning multiple Provincial gold medals. These include the Fours in 2002 as skip, Singles in 2003, and Fours again in 2004 as skip. It is interesting to listen to his story of becoming a bowler. Back in 1994, he went to watch his friend bowl in a tournament in Nanaimo. After it was finished, out of curiosity, he went down to the green and tried it himself. After throwing four bowls up and down, the president of Nanaimo LBC was amazed and said, "Have you ever bowled before? I thought you were an experienced bowler." Then he invited Hiren to join the club in the coming year when the bowling season started again.

So in 1995, he joined Nanaimo LBC and took lessons from Betty Hodgins. In the months of May and June, he went to the club everyday and entered all competitions. It was only two months after he started bowling that Harvey Hodgins took him to play the Provincial Pairs.

He remembered vividly the first Provincial game he ever played. The opponents were the ever-famous Ted Waterston and Dale Haggerty. When they walked down to the green, Harvey asked him to be the skip. "Just do what I tell you to do," he said. But of course, it was not as easy as he said. At the 6th end, the score was 9:2 to Ted. Then, in the next end, Hiren was holding four in the head. He was so happy, thinking he could draw in to score more. But in no time, Ted threw the bowl and took the jack to the back to win a bundle. "How can he make a shot like that?" was his question to Harvey. Eventually they lost the game 6 to 28.

"This was my first baptism of Provincial bowling," he said with sarcasm.

But he learnt. In 1996, Hiren went to play the Provincial Pairs again. This time his partner was the 85-year-old Frank Clevette. The first game was against Jim Murphy and Brad Neave. After playing five ends, Hiren was down at 11 to 1. Then there came an end where Jim Murphy only had one bowl in the head.

"Nobody told me what to do. I just took that bowl out and scored five. When we came to the 15th end, the score was 11 to 11. Then I scored one point onward. Finally, I won the game by two points."

Hiren has a very good memory and retains everything in detail, which might account for his success in games playing. He is a born athlete and plays nearly all sports such as soccer, rugby, table tennis, field hockey, softball, volleyball, badminton and even games such as darts and poker. He was also a champion in 400-metre track running in school.

"My advantage is to see and to make shots other people don't see. I've developed a reputation for possessing the dangerous last bowl because I always make my last bowl count. I'm very determined and I never give up. In a game, I give my best to win," said Hiren with lots of confidence in himself.

A lot of good bowlers are good seemingly because they get a leg-up from being good at other sports. But in fact, there are a lot of good bowlers who are just born bowlers. Sheila Buttar, the many-time National champion, is a natural in this sense. Her parents were very good bowlers. She started bowling over forty years ago in her 20's. She was good at it right from the start and won the novice singles that year. She is one of the very few bowlers I know of who never practices.

"I find throwing bowls by myself very boring. I only play in games. But I watch other people bowl. My mind is like a computer: when I observe, store all the memory in my mind and when I play I know what to do and I can do it well."

Sheila is not boasting. She is the one who, after resting from bowling for six months in the winter, can draw right on the jack with her very first bowl in the first game of the season. I know she is truly observant because after meeting me on the green in singles for so many years, she can tell the difference between my second set of bowls and my first set. She even seems to understand more how they work than I do.

Is it true that there is no need to practice? Dave Brown, as a coach, stressed that no matter how good you are, practice is always important. It is because there is always room for improvement. There is a saying "When you are through improving, you are through." Maybe some talented bowlers pick up bowling naturally without people telling them what to do; others learn and improve bowling by following good instructions.

Choice of Bowls - The Size and Weight

Let's look at this sport from the basics. Bowls, the instrument we use to play, come in different sizes, weights and biases. It is interesting to see how people make their choice. What kind of bowls do you pick? Craig Wilson said that when he coached the juniors, the choice of bowls would not be something to focus on. As long as they can hold the bowl and feel comfortable, that is the right bowl for them. It looks simple.

You pick up the size of the bowl which suits your hand, but how about the weight? Heavy? Or medium? Which is better?

Graham Jarvis, an engineer, is very mathematical in the art of bowling. He calculated that the medium-weight bowls work better than heavies in northern hemisphere greens. And his theory was confirmed as 100% correct by Bruce R. Hensell, the managing director of leading bowls maker Henselite.

In a letter to a bowler in the United States, Mr Hensell wrote, "It has always been the recommendation of our company that medium-weight bowls should be used on greens in the United States because, with the exception of a few greens only, their speeds are very slow."

"The finish of a bowl is relative to the rate at which it slows down at the end of its run. A heavy bowl on a slow green pulls up quickly because the extra friction of the grass slows the bowl down at a quicker rate as the heavier bowl digs into the ground more than a light weight bowl. On the other hand on a very fast green a heavy bowl runs on further as the momentum of the bowl towards the end of its run is greater than the friction of the faster grass surface and hence the bowl does not slow down as quickly. If you related this to playing bowls on the carpet in your home as to playing on an ice skating rink I think you will then understand the logic of what I am saying."

In this letter, he also had some advice on the size of the bowls.

"The sale of size 7 and 6 bowls has diminished dramatically, in fact we have ceased production of size 7 and the size 6 is very minimal. Yes, you may have a big hand but the most important thing is can you hold the bowl under all bowling conditions comfortably without strain. The bowl should be a natural extension of your arm, not something that is clamped by your fingers under pressure which affects the touch of your bowl on delivery. Most bowlers strain with big bowls."

Different Bias Bowls

It is the choice between different bias bowls which excites discussions among bowlers.

When I first started bowling in Hong Kong 17 years ago, the standard Henselite Classic bowls was the only choice. Then in recent years, many different brands of bowls designed by different manufacturers are coming to light.

It is obvious that if the bowls run straighter, they can get to the jack more easily than those which have to take a wide bend. But why do a lot of top bowlers still stay with their full bias bowls? Dave Brown uses the same set of bowls - full bias Henselite for 46 years. Bob Scott always uses the same set of bowls - size 6 full bias brand. Even when he went to bowl in the Indoor Mixed Pairs Tournament in Belfast, he refused to change to narrow bias bowls as suggested.

Sheila Buttar likes wide drawing bowls and she has used the same set for 25 years. She only changes to Classic II when playing indoor. She even sold to John Aveline a set of old bowls which she bought from a garage sale.

"This is a set of Henselite size 3 bowls manufactured in 1958. It is said that around the years in late 50's and early 60's, they produced the best drawing bowls," John said. "I like using them. Although they look so old, yet they work well on fast or heavy greens, and are just good all-purpose bowls. My wife Cathie also got a set of used bowls called Vitalite manufactured in 1954, and she got those from the club in Ontario. I remember a few years ago, we we bowling in the Pacific Indoor Open Pairs. There was a game we bowled against Vince Sutherland, the champion indoor bowler who likes to analyze the art of bowling. Cathie bowled so well with this set of bowls that Vince couldn't help but call us the day after asking about what brand of bowls she had been using."

"He didn't believe that it was me who bowled well," added Cathie. "It's the bowler, not the bowls."

The favourite bowls for the old timers are Henselite Regular Classic. Marlene Cleutinx has been for 15 years using the same bowls, the Henselite Classic size 5 heavy. Jim Aitken also uses size 5 Henselite Classics, or sometimes size 6 Greenmasters because he likes wider bias with true arc. For indoors, he turns to the narrow bias Greenmaster Proline. Nick Watkins uses Henselite Classic for outdoors and Classic II indoors. Steve Forrest had tried different kinds of bowls from full bias to minimum bias in the last 20 years. Now he uses Drakes Pride Professional because he thinks they work well on different surfaces. German Santana, a Provincial gold medalist, used Greenmaster before, and now also changes to Drakes Pride size 3 heavy for indoors as well as outdoors. He thinks Drakes Pride has a natural drawing line and holds the line better. Keith Roney uses Taylor Ace because it has a gradual bending arc. When talking about narrow bias bowls, he mentions that a new brand called "Dreamline" is being manufactured by Henselite, and another upcoming brand straighter than the ABT2000 will be called "Redline."

Narrow Bias Bowls

So how straight is a bowl allowed to roll in competition? There is certainly concern out there that some bowls are too straight to be proper lawn bowls. In the 2000 Women World Bowl, for instance, a petition was made concerning a set of bowls which subsequently after testing were disallowed. Same thing happened to Alice Duncalf once.

When Alice first started bowling, she used the standard Henselite Classic bowls. In 1982, when she was bowling in Australia, she watched some bowlers doing well with the minimum bias Taylor bowls. So she ordered a set of these Taylor bowls and eventually received it in 1986. She had used that set of bowls since and bowled very well with them. But in 1992, when she was in World Bowl, they failed the testing and had to be taken back by the manufacturer for alteration.

Henselite manufactures the Classic II which is narrower running and hook-in at the finish. Christie Grahame says he had tried different bowls before, but now stays with Classic II for outdoor and ABT2000 or Taylor Vector indoor. Graham Jarvis has also been using Henselite Classic II size 6 medium for all these years.

So, the narrows all the way? Alan Webster is a believer of narrow bias bowls. In fact, he won the Singles gold medal in 1999 Asia Pacific Games in Kuala Lumpur by using ABT2000. But he never forgets how ABT2000 has its limitations. A year later, when he played the Provincial Pairs with Tom Rosario in Victoria, both of them used this same brand of narrow bias bowls. They bowled well in the semi-final. But the final game was on a different rink with runs in the middle part of the green. Their bowls were not agreeable with the green at all and they lost the game badly. Now wherever he goes, he always carries two sets of bowls, a Henselite ABT2000 and a Classic II. After trial ends, he then decides on using which set of bowls.

Reasons for the Choice

Those in favour of full bias bowls hold the same reason: It is better for skips to use them because they can get round the front bowls and apply more variety shots. In this sense narrow bias bowls sometimes have their limitations. But honestly speaking, narrow bias bowls often maintain the advantage. To my observation, beginners bowl more easily with narrow bias bowls. My lead partners in recent years seem to prove it. Josephine Lee, who is my partner in Provincial games, uses Taylor International. Belle Chan, who plays with me in the V&D Pairs, uses Henselite Emerald, and Mary Wright, who plays lead for me in some mixed events, uses Taylor Ace. They bowl well as leads and all are very good singles players. Not only leads, there are skips who like to use narrow bias bowls. If full use is made of its narrow nature of running, they can work wonders in opening up a big head or trailing the jack to the back. Steve Forrest mentioned that Ted Waterston was a great believer in straight bowls. I remember I had seen Ted execute such skills as well. With perfect weight, he could hit squarely on the front bowl to push on another to the jack. This kind of shot would be difficult to make with a full bias bowl.

But undeniably, full bias bowls require more skill and variety of shots, which is the true art of bowling. They can get round or go inside the front bowls, wick the inside or outside part of the front bowls to get into the head, push a side bowl or basically anything a veteran bowler can think of.

That is why Dorothy Macey only uses full bias bowls. She thinks that the narrow bias bowls take a lot of skills out of the sport. Laila Hassan agrees, "I always use the same set of bowls - Henselite Classic size 4 heavy. I don't need narrow bias bowls. With skill you can make the bowl go narrower. For example, a little more weight would do it. I can also change the position on the mat or change the way of holding the bowl."

Ryan Bester thinks the same. He uses Taylor Lignoid with traditional full bias. "It's no fun to throw straight bowls," he says. "It is getting round the front objects that adds more fun and challenge which I enjoy."

So, what brand of bowls to choose? Both Dorothy Macy and Sheila Buttar say, "Good bowlers can bowl with any brand of bowls."

Dave Brown puts it this way, "We don't have different types of bowls, only different types of bowlers. Use your set of bowls no matter what brand they are. Know how they work and then work them well."

The Grip and Delivery

So you pick up the brand of bowl you like. Now how to hold it? What is the grip? Both Dave Brown and Graham Jarvis favour the "cradle grip."

"If you hold the bowl too tight, there is tension. It is better to cradle your bowl. Then you can have a better feel for it. You only hold the bowl tight when driving." Dave said.

Graham thinks that finger grip is better for bowling indoor or in the southern hemisphere with fast greens. For greens in the northern hemisphere, the cradle grip is better.

Jim Aitken, a champion bowler, when talking about gripping, said that whatever you feel comfortable, that is the best one for you. When he throws his bowls, he would massage the bowl or weigh the bowl. Feeling comfortable, he then releases it.

How about the delivery? People say that lawn bowling is one of the easiest sports to learn to play. But what is the best way to do it? Craig Wilson said that he taught the juniors the standard delivery – the Australian model.

"But they all develop differently because the body build is different. I teach them the same at start. They can work out the rest. I tell them, the mat is the place everything happens. If you step on the mat, doing the same thing and always looking for consistency, then you can bowl well."

Sheila Buttar, having a natural delivery, also says the same thing. "There is no fixed form for everybody. As long as you are happy with your own form, do the same thing every time, then it is the right form for you."

Christie Grahame, the National champion and National Team member, started bowling about 18 years ago. It was his colleague Bert Walker who first introduced him to the game. Bert used to run the Pacific Indoor LBC and bowled in the World Bowl in Australia at that time.

"I was taught to deliver in the standard way from the start - to crouch, step forward, and swing my arm. But now I've changed my delivery. When I stand on the mat, I only step forward slightly - as little movement as possible. I put the elbow down and push the arm. This way, I can get the line correctly. It works very well on fast green. And I have no problem bowling like this on heavy green because I have strength."

When you watch a video or pictures showing the standard form, you just wish you could do the same because they are good to look at. Just like when fashion shows exhibit the beauty of clothing on the body of a model. Most of us don't have the model's figure to wear clothes as good-looking as they do. And yet we do wear clothes that fit our own bodies and look good.

Some bowlers really have very funny ways of delivery. Jim Aitken recalls the strangest delivery he has ever seen was Keith Shaw's. When he was only a fourth-year bowler, he went to Victoria to play in the "Shaw Indoor Singles" Tournament. His opponent was the great bowler — Keith Shaw himself.

"Keith had a very funny way of delivery," Jim recalled. "He only put one foot on the mat. He faced sideway when holding the bowl, like a baseball pitcher. Then he turned 90 degree round, swirling the hand to send out the bowl. In spite of the awkward way of delivery, he bowled really well and beat me soundly."

"At that time, the ruling was that you must have both feet on the mat at delivery. So I went to the umpire to complain about his foot faulting. After the umpire had a word with him, he changed his delivery with two feet on the mat. But he still played well and beat the hell out of me."

How did the great bowler David Bryant talk about his own delivery?

He wrote, "I sight my line and get the feel of length and pace from a squatting position. Having got these lined up, I rise to the height necessary to allow my left front leg to shuffle forward the required distance, my swing going back in harmony with this step. The length of the backswing is adjusted to the pace of the green and the needs of the immediate shot; on fast greens it scarcely passes my back leg. Then as my left leg takes my weight I swing forward, making sure that my bowl is delivered right on the ground [well grounded]. I take great care of the follow-through, letting the arm travel well forward and keeping my head and shoulders down till long after the bowl has left my head."

For people who lose their balance in delivery, Dave Brown has this advice. "Try to take smaller steps," he said. "This is because in this way, you won't lose your balance."

It works with handicapped people like Peter Holt, the man with "two feet short." He said that when he first started bowling, he had trouble in the delivery. Then Jim Aitkin advised him to try smaller steps and he bowled very well by following this advice.

David Bryant in his book "Bowls with Bryant" explained more on this subject.

"The length of the step will vary with the propulsion and speed of delivery, but I feel it is best for the player to concentrate on swing rather than step as the latter is invariably sympathetic to the former."

"I firmly believe that many players confuse themselves by paying too much attention to length of step when bowling under conditions that they find difficult. Their deliveries often become jerky and erratic but had their concentration been placed on length of backswing closely allied to speed of action, the forward step would have been automatically of the correct length and would have been in sympathy with the other two."

"Therefore, on heavier greens a longer step and backswing will be needed with a much faster action. On fast greens the bowler will take a short step with little backswing and a slow delivery, keeping as low as possible."

"Every player has a speed of green that suits his own particular style and invariably when he encounters such a surface he immediately settles down and gives of his best. From bowler to bowler this pace will vary to suit the individual's physique and technique. Therefore, it can be said that each player has a natural height of stance, a natural swing, a natural step and a natural speed of delivery."

"When encountering conditions ideal to his or her style, a player is almost certainly going to be at peak form. The beauty of the game of bowls is that no two greens are alike and therefore adaptability is the key to success."

Line and Weight

Skill-wise, there are really only two things in bowling - line and weight. How does one get the right line? When Craig Wilson coached the juniors, the first thing he did was to get them to aim at pecks on the bank. "Then I would use anything on the green for the line. Sometimes I put coins on the green and let them roll the bowls on the coins. Kids have good eyes. This way they can get the line well."

Keith Roney, when first started, also used something on the bank for aiming, such as a boundary mark. But now he looks for some visible mark on the green. Doreen Creaney, the former National Team member, looks at about ten feet out in front of her in the grass. "I test with the first bowl and adjust with the second bowl. Some greens are regular draws both sides, some greens might run straighter because of the ridge. Then I would change my position on the mat. I would stand on the front corner of the mat instead of on the back of the mat."

Laila Hassan doesn't use any physical aiming point for line adjustment. She looks at the jack first to decide the distance. Then she estimates how the bowl would bend and decide which point is the shoulder. She would look at the imaginary shoulder for the line.

Dorothy Macey seems to have mastered this mental visualization of the line. When she steps on the mat, she visualizes the path and how the bowl would turn before she actually throws the bowl.

"You must see it before you can play it," she said.

She remembers many years ago going to a training camp at the Indoor Club in Victoria, run by Jimmy Davison. There was an exercise in which they would look at the jack first, and then they had to throw bowls blindfolded. She could roll the bowls right up to the jack because she could visualize vividly in her mind how the bowl would go. For weight control though, she thinks this cannot be taught, you just have to feel it.

Keith Roney agrees, "The weight control is from the mind to the hand. It's the feeling. Reading the green is important. In the first few ends, I try to get to know the green as quickly as possible and to keep in mind the irregularity."

One of the interesting challenges of outdoor bowling is the ever-changing green. Jim Aitken also said, "I love outdoor bowling because the green varies. When I walk up and down on the green, my feet feel for the depressions - the unevenness of the ground. I am aware of what's underneath. I collect all such information. When I throw my bowls, I know how to adjust the weight and line."

Craig Wilson also said the same thing. "Getting the weight control is all in the mind. Your hand has to do the follow through. Then focus on muscle memory. You have to practice natural length. When I coach the juniors, I don't give them the jack. They just throw bowls to get the natural length and weight."

Not only the juniors, but the world's top bowlers do the same thing. Dave Brown mentioned once that he talked to the coach of the South African Team about how they prepare for games. Apparently they just stand on the mat and keep on rolling the bowls just like a machine. Just ignore what you see. Concentrate on the feeling of the arm. When you get the consistent groove line on the green, sooner or later you can make any shots you like."

Practice Makes Perfect

"People used to ask if I did any training and I had to explain, Yes, twice a day, six times a week," a Paralympics gold medalist said during the opening ceremony of the 12th Paralympic Games in Athens.

It is true that practice makes perfect. Steve Forrest reminisces that twenty years ago, he was so keen to be a champion bowler that he practiced every day. He even went into a structured practice routine by keeping score cards. He remembers when the indoor facility in Victoria was first built, he practiced to the extent that he could make adjustment of a quarter of an inch.

Christie Grahame recalls that when he first started bowling, he practiced at least three or four times a week.

"I work hard to bowl well," he said. "When I practice, I play for the shot and also practice different lengths. I also go into a lot of competitions. I don't mind bowling with new bowlers and I just go for the experience."

Alan Webster says that he needs to practice. When he practices, he uses the format of different drills. Jim Aitken says that he won't over- practice. Usually he only practices for six to eight ends. If he practices more than he feels, it becomes labour which would spoil the fun.

"There are different ways of practicing the skill," Dave Brown said. "Whatever method you use, you must enjoy your practice. Skill is part of the game. You also have to practice to look at the head. When I was playing in the county in England at seventeen, I was trained to read the head. When you look at the head, you have to memorize it. Focus on what you remember and apply the skill."

Practice makes perfect

Watch Games and Go into Competition

Bill Boettger, a National Coaching Certification Program level coach, has been serving the National Team as such for a long time. How did he improve his own game?

"I read bowls materials, got involved in both the bowls coaching program and the umpiring program," he said. "I tried to analyze each loss and learn from it."

Then he stressed that the best ways to improve are to watch games and to go into competition. "I watched and learned from the good players, particularly concerning game strategies. Best way of all is to go out to play. Before, being a school teacher, I had two months in the summer to play competitive bowls every Saturday, Sunday, Wednesday as well as two week-long tournaments (WOBA and PLBT). These matches were against the best Ontario had to offer and we traveled all over the province to compete."

Sheila Buttar also learned by watching games. She remembers when her mother played in the World Bowl in 1976, she went to watch the games. By observing the top bowlers' games, she learnt how to make the shots. Dorothy Macey also thinks that the best way to improve your game is to go and watch good bowlers play their games.

"In those days, I liked to go to Stanley Park LBC to watch those top men bowlers bowl. When I watched the head, I would think to myself what I would do to make the shot. Then I watched how they did it. After the game, I would ask them why they made such shots. The even better way to improve is to go into competition beyond your club. You do not learn much staying in the club to play with social bowlers. In those days, I didn't mind going into big games and getting wiped out.

I continued to go and get wiped out until I played well myself. Unless you play against the best bowlers, you don't improve."

That is true. The more competitive the game, the more you can learn because you can have the chance to play against good bowlers. They are your best teachers. Also, a good opponent can bring the best out of you.

I remember an interesting incident when I was playing in the Atlantic Rim Games in Wales in 1997 where 14 countries played on a round-robin basis for two whole weeks.

The Dutch bowling team, coming from a very small bowling community with little competitive bowling, was considered the weakest team of all. They only produced large scores in the oppositions' favour. But after playing two games or sometimes three games per day for over ten days against top bowlers, they improved tremendously. When they came to play the Fours game against the defending champion - Scotland, to everyone's surprise, they beat Scotland 17 to 15. The Scottish team was stunned by such totally unexpected result. When we were having breakfast the morning after, the table for Scottish team was empty. The coach was probably having a word with the whole team. When the Dutch old ladies walked into the dining room, we all clapped hands and cheered them. The poor Scottish team, if not for this defeat, would probably been in the highest ranking. They ended up only getting a bronze medal.

Those who play in competitive bowling - win or lose - learn a lot. Most important of all, they can taste the sensation of the competitiveness of the game which is the real fun of bowling.

Chapter 3

Fire or Draw and the Strategy Involved

Ω

Draw

WHAT IS THE WORD you most commonly hear on the green? Yes, you are right. It is "draw." When the lead starts to throw the bowl, the skip would say "draw". When they are holding shots in the head, you also hear the word "draw". Even when they are down in the head, the word you often hear is still - "draw". After all, this is a drawing game.

I remember in 1999, I bowled in the Atlantic Rim Games in Cape Town, South Africa. We went there a few days earlier to prepare ourselves for the game. The local clubs were kind enough to bring us to their greens to practice. We were fortunate to have a chance to bowl in the beautiful Glen Country Club located along the beach under the famous Twelve Apostles Mountains facing the magnificent Ocean. During a game of triples, I found their skip was playing a very finesse game. No matter what the situation of the head, this old gentleman only drew to the head. I couldn't help but ask the opposing lead, "How come your skip never throws a runner? This head looks so easy to smash. Our men at home would probably go for a driving shot."

"Our skip believes in drawing," he smiled and said. "He thinks that male bowlers play a driving shot just to show off and attract the attention of lady spectators."

Although he didn't throw driving shots to impress us, he did impress us with beautiful drawing shots. He just beat us by simply drawing to the jack.

Nick Watkins, one of Canada's top indoor players, went to bowl in two professional events in 2002 after winning the PBA qualifying matches in Canada. When he was in Llanelli, Wales, he stayed behind to watch the game after losing his first match. In this championship, English legend Tony Allcock produced a remarkable farewell performance in the event as he beat the world No. 1, Gourlay, 12-2, 8-1 to collect the £10,000 first prize.

"We were fortunate to be at the tournament to watch Tony Allcock play in his last major championship, which he won by defeating David Gourlay soundly in the final," said Watkins.

"The bowling was impressive, and the message was simple - you must be a master of the draw shot in order to achieve success at this level."

Fire

It is true that you can win a game by drawing and drawing. The point is to dead draw to the jack, especially on the outdoor greens, and with different circumstances that is the most difficult shot. At least, there is no luck involved. On the other hand, honestly speaking, the vigorous and stimulating firing shot is exciting to watch.

When I was a first-year bowler, I knew very little about lawn bowling. Then I got a chance to watch the top bowlers playing in the final Singles game of the Hong Kong Classic Tournament. This annual invitational event is usually held in late November and features some of the best singles players from all over the world.

The final game was between an Australian bowler, the defending champion, and a local bowler. Whenever the Hong Kong bowler was right on the jack with his bowl, the Australian just fired at it. The bowl shot out like a bullet. "Bang" and the head was burnt. He repeated this again and again until the Hong Kong bowler was not that close. Then he drew his bowl

Are you out of your mind?! I asked you to "fire" with your bowl, not to shoot with the machine gun !

near the jack to score. It was an eye opener for me and it was the first time I knew lawn bowling could be played like this.

Firing shots is appealing especially to non-bowlers. Jim Murphy recalls his experience of watching a bowling match when he knew nothing about lawn bowling. Many years ago, he lived near the Vancouver South LBC. One day, he walked by the club and saw a crowd there watching a game. Out of curiosity, he also stayed there as a spectator. It was Dave Duncalf and Jim Morrison playing against an outside team in the final game of the Gold Medallion. When the game came to the last end, Jim Morrison was down five points. Then he kept burning the head four times till he got six points and won the game. "It was unbelievable and fascinating. That's how I was attracted to lawn bowling," he said.

The Favourite Shot

When should you drive and when should you draw? What about the other skillful shots? What is your favourite shot?

"The draw is my favourite shot," Sheila Buttar said. "But I also like the wick-in shot. People may say that I count on luck. But actually this is part of the skill."

Christie Grahame also thinks that drawing is his best skill. He said, "To be a good bowler, you have to be a good draw bowler. I also like the take-out shots - but take-out with controlled weight. My decision to do certain shots depends on the setup of the head. Very often I would play yard-on shots. There are times that I have to take extra weight to burn the head. Another favourite shot is promoting, I make use of the position of the front bowls and raise them to the head."

Alan Webster also says that he draws as much as he can and he only drives in desperate situation. He fires with the intention to burn the head. He doesn't believe in blocker and puts position bowls instead.

Dave Brown said, "I don't recall I ever drove in international events. Don't drive indiscriminately. But when you do, it's better to aim at the bowls rather than the jack. In any case, the strength is to draw to the position, not to drive."

How about the skips? What should be their favourite shots? Alice Duncalf said, "When it comes down to the skip, draw may not be there. As the game goes on, you have to use weight to wick in or get in, but not those forceful firing shots. When you are in serious trouble, you must take any chance to draw in to cut down before firing. I don't believe in blockers because you can only block one side. I put position bowls instead of blockers. My secret of winning is to change the head, tucking the jack and making it difficult for the opponent to play."

Keith Roney explains that the Australian bowlers drive a lot because on their fast greens, it is either draw or fire. That is why Tony Allcock once said, "Firing is an important part of our game. In Australia, firing is practiced with as much importance as the draw shot."

Keith said, "I don't fire a lot. There is a saying, 'drive to show, draw to gold.' It means you drive because you want to show off, but it is the drawing shot which helps you winning games, thus winning the prize."

Although Ryan Bester, the young world champion, can throw dynamite full-blooded driving shots, he agrees with the idea. He says, "Drive to save, draw to win."

What fascinates Laila Hassan in lawn bowling is all the various skills she has to apply in order to make the shot.

"I would use different methods to make the shot," she said. "I have the talent to look at the head to decide what hand to play and what shot to make. It is just like playing billiards. All the shots provide lots of opportunity. Even when there are a lot of bowls on the green. For some people, they may find the front bowls are in their way. I look at it from another angle. All the bowls are useful. You can make use of them. They can be guide bowls or you can wick in or do promoting. Then you adjust your weight and line, the position on the mat and the holding of the bowl to tackle the problem."

How to master different skills of shots? Frank Soars in his book "The Modern Approach to Bowls" gives us a very good hint. I quote:

"There are only two types of shots in bowls: one played to an exact position on the green; the other, the faster shot which reached the ditch. The trail, the wrest, the yard-on and the two-yards-on are all draw shots. And until a player realizes this, he will have limited success with these shots."

Usually, we refer to "drawing shots" as drawing to the jack. Actually, not only the trail, wrest or yard-on shots but the blockers or position back bowls are all drawing shots to a position on the green. Unless you draw well, you cannot expect to be successful with the other shots, which are really just variations.

As to the choice of shots to make, Dave Brown believes the first thing that comes to your mind is often the best shot. "Thinking too much might not yield the right shot," he said. "Make up your mind before you step on the mat. When you do step on the mat, stick to what you've decided to do."

Dorothy Macey says the same thing, "The first instinct is the right instinct."

Possession of the Mat

There is a new rule that the winner of the preceding scoring end can have the option to either take the mat and have the jack and the first bowl, or allow the opponent to. Should you take the mat or not?

Before this new rule, the same situation usually arises in the first end or extra end when you win the toss, David Bryant suggests that for the first end, "it is perhaps better to deliver the last bowl." In the case of an extra end situation, "there is a strong argument for settling for the last bowl and giving the jack to your opponent." However, in singles, "there is good argument for taking the jack."

Ryan Bester agrees that in playing singles, he would take the jack because in this way, he can have bowls on the jack first to put pressure on the opponent. But he would take the last bowl in the last end. He said, "When I played the Pairs in World Bowl 2004, I kept the mat when I wanted to have control of the length. But when I came to the last end, I took the last bowl. There were times I saw my lead playing better than the opponent, and so I took the last bowl."

The word is not definitive, however, and theories about this keep changing. Both Keith Roney and Dave Brown were at World Bowl 2004 where it was the first year that the new rule was applied. They noticed that in the beginning, most bowlers gave away the mat. But later, for some reason, they all changed to keeping the mat.

There will continue to be debate over whether you should take the mat or not. Dave Brown is one who is all against the idea of giving the mat away. "When you get the momentum going, don't give the mat to your opponent," he said. "To give away the mat is a curling philosophy. It doesn't work in bowling. To keep the hammer is negative - thinking you have to save the head. The chance of success - getting the result you want - is less than 4%."

Although Keith Roney noticed that in World Bowl 2004, at some point the bowlers changed from giving the mat away to keeping the mat, he thinks that when you have the last bowl, you can add to the score or save the end.

Alan Webster reckons giving away the mat is better because "I'm better with my 4th bowl than my opposition with their first. Other than jack length, their only advantage is their first bowl."

Steve Forrest is all for giving the jack away and playing the last bowl because this involves more technical advantage. He says, "When you are really good, you don't mind the length - whether it is long or short, forehand or backhand. There is no unbeatable bowl if you have the skill."

Laila Hassan welcomes the new rule because to have a choice is better than no choice, which leads to more strategy. "To give away the mat can test which length your opponent likes," she believes. "If your opponent cannot draw near the jack, you better choose to have the hammer. If your opponent's first bowl is always touching the jack you better go first before she does."

An astute skip can take advantage of the situation when the mat is given. Graham Jarvis said, "We know that we should not change a winning length. If your opponents are in this situation, then you are losing at that length. So, win the end as soon as possible, take the jack, and change the length. To take the jack or not is a judgment call and will vary from one end to another."

Beryl Harrington expressed an honest opinion on this issue. She said, "All these years, I got used to possessing the jack if winning. So, if my opponent gives the mat to me, I have the feeling of winning, which is not bad. The reason for people to take the last bowl is that they believe they're so good that they can make any shot they like. Does the new rule make the game better? I don't think so. On the other hand, it does no harm to the game. It is a rule. It is there. So we have to accept it. You can use it to your advantage. But not because everybody is doing it that you have to do it."

In theory, if you are really that good to make any shot and have the confidence to make it, then you have the advantage of the last bowl. But are we as good as we think we are? Also, in outdoor bowling, there are a large number of external factors such as the conditions of the weather and the green which would affect the accuracy of making shots. Especially when it is a team situation, can all your team members adjust to a change in jack length?

There was a Provincial game I played this year that illustrates all these considerations. Our opponents were average bowlers. Yet all through the game, their skip kept giving the mat away. The green was extremely fast running. My lead, who is not used to bowling on fast greens, had obvious trouble in the weight control. When it was a full-length jack, her bowls would roll to the ditch. When it was a short jack, her bowls were at least three yards in the back. So the safest distance for us was the medium jack. But there were times when she threw the jack to the ditch and the opposing lead had to take the jack. Every time the opposing lead threw the jack it was right past the hog line. She was the only one who could manage to bowl near the jack at such length. And yet, I was relieved to see that the opposing skip, not aware of their strength, kept giving the jack back to us and saved us from bowling the short jack. You could say that was our strategic advantage and we won that game.

Actually, there is no steadfast rule in mat strategy. A lot comes from experience. It depends on the different situations. Graham Jarvis is right to say, "Strategy is variable depending upon whom you bowl against. Get to know your opponent, your own strengths and weaknesses and apply the appropriate strategy."

Talking about strategy, Beryl Harrington also said, "You have to play every single game differently. Call for different shots. Even if I can live to be a hundred and keep teaching you, I still can't show you how to apply the right strategy in every game. There are thousands of possibilities in every shot. I learn something new every time. Nobody ever knows all that is to know about lawn bowling.

That's how wonderful the sport is."

TIPS FOR SHOT SELECTION, TACTICS & PLAYING SHOTS

(Compiled by Bill Boettger from Jimmy Davidson of England, Bowls International Magazine)

1. SIMPLICITY: The easier shot is usually the right shot to play.

2. SCOREBOARD GUIDANCE: The scoreboard sometimes dictates that the conservative, or alternatively - the gambling shot, is the one to play.

3. STRENGTH & WEAKNESS: Play to your own strength and your opponent's weakness. Your best guide is your own team's performance on that day, as well as that of your opponents.

4. BEATING TOUCHERS: In singles, pairs, triples or fours, the best response to a front toucher is to get one close to cut down a possible big count but to increase your shot options on subsequent bowls. There are a variety of possibilities for using a close bowl in front, at the side or behind the jack.

5. DITCH DRAWING. With the jack in the ditch, don't draw close to the ditch with your last bowl, just draw to a point past your opponent's nearest bowl.

6. OPPOSING THOUGHT: That shot your opponents don't want you to play is usually the shot you're looking for. So put yourself in their shoes and think from their point of view.

7. LATE STAGES: Late in the game, particularly on the last end, in a straight choice between a "dead draw" and a firing shot inside: with shot against, chose the weight shot. There are usually more options for a favorable outcome to occur.

8. WHICH HAND: if both hands are equally true, choose the tighter hand, because in percentage terms, it should be easier to play.

Chapter 4

Does Personality Matter?

Ω

YOU MAY HAVE the physical prowess or technical ability, but there is always something else within which distinguishes the champion bowler from the average bowler. We all have different personalities. Some are more determined or assertive, some may be more nervous or tense. What kind of person are you? Does personality help to make a better bowler?

Calm

Sheila Buttar thinks that a good bowler must be confident, calm and have a positive attitude. As for herself, "I take things easy. If I don't do something well, I won't do it. I enjoy bowling but it is not the priority in my life."

German Santana also agrees that to be calm and to have concentration are very important. "Don't be uptight. The game is supposed to be fun. It doesn't mean I'm not serious. I'm serious on the green and determine to win."

It is natural to get uptight in a game situation. We are human after all. There is a creepy feeling in the abdomen, with short breaths during the first few ends. Even an experienced bowler like Alice Duncalf feels the same. "To some people, winning is everything," Alice said. "I don't try that hard in social games. Only for games that matter would I mean business. Before a big game, I might get edgy, and have butterflies in my stomach. It's part of me. But once the game starts, it's fine."

"People tend to be nervous." Keith Roney said. "They put pressure on themselves. You must be calm. Don't let things upset you. When I first started, I was very anxious and tense. Now, I think to myself, there's no point in worrying. A good bowler must be positive and aggressive - to take chances, not stupid chances though, of course."

Even a young bowler like Derek Kaufman says a good bowler needs to be calm. "Look at those people who win all the time. They are all consistently calm and relaxed. It doesn't mean they are relaxed in a way of laxity. They must be also very competitive."

Marlene Cleutinx, a person with great composure, thinks that patience in bowling is very important. "Don't get upset when your opponent gets a lucky wick-in. Stay calm all the time."

Graham Jarvis, another very calm and patient person, stresses that to be calm is very important. He even puts it down in his so-called "da di da" list. "Never be in a hurry to play a bad shot," he says.

He gave me an interesting example. It was in 1977, he played the final game of the Provincial Fours with Bert Corcoran as the vice. It was a close game. When it came to the second last end, they were two points up on the board but were three points down on the green. It was Bert's turn to throw his bowl. Knowing that it was a crucial moment to save the head, he became very anxious and hurriedly threw the first bowl, which did not make the shot.

"I saw that he was too anxious," Graham said. "If I didn't do something, one bad shot would follow another. So before he delivered his second bowl, I called him forward and we met in the middle of the green which slowed things down. Then I said to him, 'Which team do you think will win the Grey Cup this year?' After the initial shock of such a question, he was a smart enough guy to understand that I was trying to change his thinking process. Immediately, all his tension was removed. As he was about to return to the mat, he turned around and said with a laugh, 'Winnipeg Blue Bombers!' With his second bowl he played a super shot in a relaxed manner and he saved the end which enabled us to win the BC Provincial Fours title that year.

Quiet

Compared to other sports, lawn bowling is a quiet game. Because good bowlers need to be calm, need to concentrate, most of the time they are quiet on the green.

"When I bowl, I don't talk much to the opponent," said Sheila Buttar. "I need to concentrate. I never get mad on the green, even when my opponent behaves badly. I only play better to beat them. I am mad at things unfair and I don't believe in gamesmanship."

"A good bowler must be quiet and concentrate," Beryl Harrington also said the same thing. "Only in playing singles though," she added. "In team playing, you have to communicate with your partners. To give clear and definite instructions and words of appreciation are often helpful to the game."

In social games, and even competitive ones, some witty conversations often add to the fun of the game. Some friendly chatting might ease the tension as well.

Jim Aitkin is a talkative person. "Before a game, I try to relax and talking to other people is a way to release my tension," he said. "But there are people who are very quiet, like John Henderson. He is a very good bowler and he is very quiet on the green. I asked him once why don't you ever say a word of appreciation to me when I make a good shot. He said, 'there's no need for me to tell you. You know you have made one.'"

"I remember in 1981, when I played lead and John the second in a Provincial Fours game with Steve Forrest and Norm Broomhall. There was a head that Steve and Norm could not make up their mind as to what shot to play. I asked John, 'Why don't you speak out your opinion as you are the most experienced one in the team.' He said, 'I like to remain quiet. If they think they need my advice, they would have asked me. Don't worry, they can figure out what to do by themselves.'"

"There was only one occasion that John said something. He was playing with me in a club game. There was a head that we had five bowls right behind the jack. The opponent was laying two bowls a little bit in front of the jack with one on each side. John said to me, 'We are going to score six this end.' Then he threw his bowl. The bowl went right in the middle, splitting the two front bowls and took the jack to the back scoring six. While the two front bowls split a little bit aside, working as perfect blocker for the opponent's bowl to get in."

Fun Character

Cary Manns, who only goes for competitive bowling, thinks that a good bowler must have what he refers to as killer instinct. "The best thing is if even when you bowl aggressively, after the game, your opponent would still say, 'I'm happy to have bowled with you.' I like good bowlers with nice personality such as George Boxwell and Christie Grahame."

George Boxwell must be a character. When I asked people about funny stories on the green, some of them would mention George Boxwell, "because he has a lot of funny stories on the green." Martha Welsh told me that there was a time when George was bowling in WOBA, he was distracted by a woman showing her legs. When I asked George about the story, "It's not true," he said.

"Then, can you tell me any funny stories on the green yourself?"

After thinking for a few seconds, he told me the following story.

In the old days, George very often bowled with Jimmy Law. Jimmy had a habit to ask George to roll a gentle bowl onto the head when the opponent's bowl was a few inches in front of the jack. Jimmy would say, "Roll your bowl gently as though you are cracking an egg. C'mon, crack an egg on the bowl."

So one day, when Jimmy used the same expression, George walked up to the head and took an egg from his pocket and cracked the egg on the bowl as told.

That is the personality of George — a very funny person on the green. He is playful sometimes but enjoys bowling. He has been rated by some bowlers as one of the best bowlers in Canada.

Bob Scott, a National champion, is also a fun character. He started bowling in the 70's when he was only 15. He skipped school one day and strolled to QE Park. He watched some people play bowls in the club there. After trying, he liked it. How come a rather slow game like lawn bowling could attract an active teenager like Bob? In his own language, he describes why he enjoys bowling. "I throw the bowl with a nice draw line, suck it around the front bowl, go through a hole and take the jack. Piss the other team off. That's why I enjoy it. It is hard to explain to other people that it's a great game. People just don't understand how much fun there is."

In a Men's Saturday Triples, I interviewed Bob Scott in between the games. I asked him why people sometimes throw good bowls and sometimes bad bowls? Why the inconsistency?

"I don't know why," he answered simply. Later on, after he had finished playing a game, he walked up to me and pointed to his head with his finger. "Oh, I know the answer. Here," he kept pointing his head. "It's temporarily out of order." Obviously, he had just lost the game and had been bowling badly.

"I seldom play singles. Singles games are boring because your opponents don't talk to you. In team playing, there is somebody to talk to. I like to team up with fun people. We can enjoy a good laugh together. Some people are too serious. Losing a game is like the end of the world to them."

Positive

Beryl Harrington said that bowlers are extremely nice people. Christie Grahame is considered a very nice person by nearly everyone. How does Christie think of himself?

"I never worry and I'm never affected by who I bowl against. Even when I bowl against those world-class bowlers, I never get intimidated. I only try harder and bowl better. I always feel positive. I am easygoing. I can go for both social bowling as well as competitive bowling. I bowl to enjoy. Winning a game doesn't mean that much. I only enjoy good shots and bowl with positive people."

Laila Hassan also thinks that good bowlers must be positive. "A good bowler should be optimistic, not pessimistic," she said. "I don't like superstitious people because you have to believe in yourself rather than rely on putting some lucky charms on to help you. You have to watch out for your own body language. When something goes wrong, don't shake your head in disappointment. You should always say to yourself, 'the next one.' Give encouraging words to your partners as well as to yourself. I like to hang around with optimistic people. They have more fun. Even when losing a game, you can still have fun and be a gracious loser."

Competitive

For some people, winning isn't everything, but the will to win is. A good bowler should have the killer instinct. That's why most leading sportsmen are highly strung with this fighting characteristic. Dorothy Macey thinks that in order to be a good bowler, you must be competitive. "This competitiveness is inborn or has to be learnt early in life." She reflected that she learnt it when she was small. She has a sister who is fourteen months older. But they were brought up together just like twins. So she always had to work hard to catch up with her sister.

"There's always an inner drive to do better, a need to excel all the time. When I was training for track and field in school, I competed with myself. I tried to beat my last record, and strived to better my time in running. I feel the same in lawn bowling. That's why I am very serious on the green. When I'm serious, I frown. Maybe because of my attitude, people think I'm unapproachable and even think I am too anxious to win. That's not true. I've got lots of medals. I just throw them in the drawers. It's not the trophies or medals that are important. Winning is not that important. It's just to play the best you can - the feeling of being excellent - that is important."

Steve Forrest thinks the same. He thinks the right character in bowling is to be competitive. "To be calm, but you must have a fire burning inside - under control, of course. Some people become nasty on the green because they want to win so much. I was a nasty person once. Ten years ago, I was very serious. Bowling was literally a matter of life and death to me. When I was in the National Team, I wanted to play well for the country. When you are trying too desperately to win, you become mentally unbalanced. It's not worth it. I was not happy. You have to respect others. I didn't enjoy myself in those days. Now, I'm doing well and become more successful because I'm more relaxed and I care to improve the game technically. I enjoy the game and like myself better. Life is more fun."

Talking about personality?
Let's say bowlers all have split personality.

Buddies off the green

Enemies on the green

Yes, when people are too desperate to win, they would become mentally unbalanced and behave badly. Ted Waterston, the rebel on the green, was a typical one. I remember the very first time I met him was in the mixed pairs event - the Bronze Medallion - many years ago. He behaved arrogantly. He didn't look at me and didn't even bother to shake hands with me. "I have to beat this guy," I said to myself. I bowled my best and outdrew his partner. Then he started yelling to that poor lady. That made things become even worse and I won the game. Later on, when I got to know him better, he turned out to be a very friendly person. After which, I asked him why he behaved like that on the green.

"Yes, I like to intimidate my opponent. As to my team mates, I deliberately give pressure to them to make them bowl better," he answered.

To him, winning means everything. Just like a warrior in the battlefield, the sole mission is to beat your opponent. Also, like the movie character, Highlander, a warrior has no mercy. I remember one year, my husband CP bowled as lead for Ted in the Triples in BC Week. It was raining heavily and they bowled against a team of older men who were obviously having trouble with the heavy green. CP always has a soft spot in his heart for senior people. Since their scores were way up, CP did not throw full jack as directed. Then Ted walked up to CP and talked in a very serious tone, "I asked you to throw a long jack, then you have to throw a long jack."

Actually, off the green, Ted was a very funny guy. He used to be in a rock band and could be very entertaining. As a nonconformist, he also fought against establishment and behaved badly just for the sake of protesting. He always enjoyed to surprising people in all sort of unexpected ways, especially with the way he looked. He told me that way back in the old days in Scotland, he was warned by the club authority to put on proper clothing.

"So I went to the club on the next day. To everyone's surprise, I dressed in a tuxedo" Ted laughed mischievously, enjoying the prank he made.

Dave Brown, a completely different person from Ted, looks at competitive bowling from another angle. "When I won the club singles at eleven, my father told me, 'Never take yourself too seriously. It's only a game.' To lose a game is not something devastating. If someone bowls better than you, so be it. There is no need to be depressed. It is no big deal. I think the excitement of the sport is being able to prepare for a game, not knowing who that person is, when there's no preconceived idea of the game and the opponent is better. There is no fun if you know you'll win a game. It is the unknown part which is interesting."

Then he added, "To be a good bowler, you better have a sense of humor."

Beryl Harrington said that lawn bowling is not only a sport, it is a way of life. She said, "If the worst thing that happens to you is losing a game, that means you're a fortunate person because there are much worse things that can happen in life."

Different Characters

We all have different character. Bowlers sometimes act differently on the green and off the green. Which one is their true self?

The bowling community can be compared to a natural garden with different species of flowers and plants. Some flowers have beautiful colours, some have sweet smell and some may have thorns. All these only add to the variety and make the garden more interesting. Just like various brands of temperaments - the fighting or determined species, the inferiority complex assortment, the nervous and irritating, also the suspicious, self-conscious variety.

Throughout the years I have been a bowler, I get to know so many different kinds of people. Some are cheerful, some are hot-tempered, some are playful and some are serious. Somehow, even when a few of them are no longer with us, each one of them has his or her own peculiarity and becomes part of my memory. We always enjoy bowling with nice people. But don't we sometimes have extra fun in beating those unpopular ones?

Simon Cowell, one of the judges of the popular television show American Idol, is famous for giving blunt and harsh comments on the contestants. He was named by "Times" as one of the most influential people in the entertaining world.

"What the show understands and the music biz often doesn't," says Simon Cowell, "is that it's personalities, it's conflict, it's all of those things that actually make [performers] interesting."

Maybe we can say the same about lawn bowling. It's personalities, it's conflict, it's all these things that actually make lawn bowling interesting.

Tips for Self-Motivation & Positive Thought

(Compiled by Bill Boettger from Jimmy Davidson of England, Bowls International Magazine)

1. SELF-PSYCHING: The kid playing practice soccer has got it right when he says, "this kick could win the World Cup." That is the right self-psyching attitude not only for practice but before you play the big shots in competition.

2. CONCENTRATION: In a fours game, you'll stand on the mat for only about 3% of the game. Keep your deepest concentration for those precious seconds.

3. CONFIDENCE: Every bowler knows that it is easier to draw a fifth scoring shot than it is to draw shot with four against. When you are four down with one bowl to play, try not to see anything but the jack for that vital draw. Ignore the four scoring bowls.

4. RELAXEZ-VOUS: The perfect competition condition is to have a concentrating mind in a relaxed body.

5. IGNORE HISTORY: The hardest lesson to learn is that the only bowl that should be in your mind is the next one - especially if the last one wasn't that good. Previous bowls are history.

6. FORGET FLUKES: When an opponent gets a fluke you can actually see some players letting it upset them. They then mentally rehearse telling their mates after the game about the fluke that beat them and it almost always becomes a self-fulfilling prophesy. The most positive way to react is to laugh at it, then put it out of your mind and think of other things.

7. EXPEL FAILURE: Be positive - don't allow fear of failure to enter your mind when on the mat - failure thrives on a mind that fears it. If you find yourself thinking about the consequences of missing, then concentrate on the mechanics of playing the shot well rather than the possible outcome.

Chapter 5

The Test of a True Sportsperson – Singles

Ω

On Your Own

I LIKE PLAYING SINGLES because it is challenging. It is a lonely game like life itself. You have to live every moment by yourself. No one can replace you.

Sheila Buttar is a many-time National Singles champion and the first woman in BC to win the open Shaw Indoor Singles Tournament. She said, "I am a loner because I am the only child in the family. I enjoy playing singles because I am a very independent person. I like to be on my own - happy to do things by myself. For example I enjoy going to the gallery alone."

Dave Brown likes singles also because he can be on his own. "It all comes down to your individual skill. There's no need for me to take other people into consideration," he said. "To play singles, you have to be single-minded with a little bit of conceit - self-belief in your own ability."

Lead or skip

I played skip very early in my bowling career. When I came to Canada and became more ambitious to play in big events, I concentrated on playing lead for two years - throwing a good jack and polishing my drawing skill. Later on, I started to play skip again all because I believe in order to play singles well, you have to have skip shots to win. In fact, most world singles champions are skips. When I bowled in the Atlantic Rim Games in 1998, I was the only singles player who played lead in other events. I remember the game I played against the world top women singles player Margaret Johnson. I played my best. We had a back-and-forth battle with the score tied on several occasions. Then there was an end that my first two bowls were right on the jack. Then Margaret, without any hesitation,

Singles is a lonely game

threw a firing shot and burnt the head. After that end, she was deadly and prevailed over me by 25 to 21. That is how you can win a singles game when you have skip shots.

Alice Duncalf also thinks that a skip makes a better singles player because you have to know all the shots. But Marlene Cleutinx thinks that a lead makes a better singles player because singles is a drawing game. To play lead is also a drawing game.

Christie Grahame also thinks that a good lead makes a better singles player because he thinks the secret of singles playing is to draw. Drawing to the jack or drawing to a position is what you need to win. He said, "Even when your opponent is touching the jack, don't drive. Only when you have a 2nd or 3rd, then fire. Try to avoid losing more than one. When I was younger, I usually tried a variety of shots. But now, only draw for the shot."

"Singles is basically a drawing game," said Dave Brown. "You must be selective in driving. When you drive, you leave yourself vulnerable. You must get bowls in position."

Jack Length

Alice Duncalf, a good skip as well as a good singles player, thinks it's important in singles to have control of the length. "Don't give away the jack," she said. "I love to throw the jack - to get the weight. I feel my weight with the jack and have the confidence. I also try to find out my opponent's favourite length. If I get the same length well, I would keep it. To throw the jack gives you the control."

Sheila Buttar said she bowls better on a faster green. The secret of winning singles is to play in her favourite length - the short jack, especially the hog line jack. That's why she also likes to have the jack in her control. She said, "If I win the toss,

I would always go first, to have control of the game. Don't give away the control of the game to your opponent."

"To win the end, continue to control the length." Dave Brown also said, "so you can keep up with the consistency. With the mat, I can play some tactics. I would move the mat a bit up or a bit down to confuse my opponent. But no matter where I put the mat, I throw the jack with the same length. When I am in control of the jack, I'm deadly with my first bowl, which would intimidate my opponent."

How to Win

Bill Boettger thinks that Singles is too lonely. Although he prefers pairs or fours to singles, he won the first match when he played the 1988 World Indoor Singles in Coatbridge, Scotland, and he won a silver medal in singles - lost to Noel Kennedy in the 1994 Hong Kong Classic.

"In singles, always try to get second shot," he said. "You must 'tramp the green.' I've seen many singles lost because a player doesn't go to the head and see the lay. Find the good side and play it come hell or bowls in the way. Vary the pace of the game to your advantage." Then he added, "Of course, score the last end."

Alice Duncalf said, "In playing singles, you have to concentrate, which is essential to winning the game. Watch your opponent's bowls. Know how their bowls react and find out their weaknesses. Confidence is also important other than concentration."

Sheila Buttar also thinks that concentration is essential. She said, "I don't talk much to the opponent, because I have to watch every bowl my opponent throws and remember how it works. Also, you have to be quick to find out which is the best hand. There are times when I can't find out which hand is best. Those are the games I don't play well."

"In singles, I apply different strategies," Hiren Bhartu said. "I assess my opponent early enough to do anything necessary to beat him. If it is meant to be a drawing game, I draw. If it's a game that you have to make percentage shots, I would make various skillful shots. Basically, I am quick to adapt to win. After a couple ends, I can decide what to play. My assessment comes quickly and I can play different strategy."

Dave Brown thinks positively in how to apply strategy in singles. He said, "Usually, I don't care what my opponent's weakness or strength is. I focus on the best I can do myself rather than playing to the weakness of my opponent."

Graham Jarvis is a good example of playing his strength in singles. He would usually take the mat up to the centre of the green and throw the jack on the six-foot mark. In this way, the inexperienced bowler might find many of his bowls in the ditch, much to his chagrin. In an effort to correct this, he would probably start dropping short. Graham beat a lot of people with this strategy. Even Christie Grahame mentioned that in the beginning, he usually practiced playing long jacks because that is the favourite length of most men players. When one day he lost badly to Graham in a game of singles, then he started to practice playing short jack.

"I learnt this from reading David Bryant's book," Graham explained. "I find it a good strategy. With experience, I can do it well with good weight control. Actually, this is only one of the strategies. I don't necessary apply the same strategy every time. Strategy is variable depending on who you bowl against."

Neil Hunter is one of the top singles players who won Provincial Singles even when she was over 70 years old. She was also famous for playing short jack. With perfect weight control, she even manages to throw the jack exactly at the 70' mark every time. Her secret of winning is simple. She told me, "Always draw, avoid firing shots. Always pick the shortest way to the jack and practice hard to play up shots with not a yard's weight, but a foot's weight or even 6 inches' weight."

I had the good fortune to bowl with her in the Pairs in BC Week before she retired from bowling. She was quick to find out the best hand to play. With great control of line and weight, she bowled like a machine. She showed me what a good draw bowler should be.

The most amazing strategy I ever learnt is from the great woman singles player, the late Dorothy Foreman. When I first met her many years ago, she was over 90 years of age and was still winning the Indoor singles. At that time, I had a chance to watch how she bowled. We all think that the important thing in playing singles is drawing to the jack. Not Dorothy. The jack was not her only target. She gained the tactical advantage by beating her opponent's bowl. In this way, no matter how the jack is moved, she would still have the chance to hold the shot. Moreover, she would win big enders if the opponent could not draw nearer.

Memorable Games

I always remember those singles games in which I played against good bowlers. What are your memorable singles games?

"I've got quite a number of memorable singles games," said Bill Boettger. "In the 1994 Canadian final, I played against Mark Gilliland. I counted 4 the first end, 4 the second end and was lying 4 on the third end when he fluked shot on a rub. The game continued and, as the sun became hotter, the green speeded up to the point where my bowls were out of control. He beat me easily in the end."

"I've had two memorable semi-final Ontario Championship Games that stand out," he continued. "In 1989, against Dan Milligan in Woodstock, we played for 4 hours and I finally lost 25-24. The other was against Ron Jones in 1995, also a lengthy battle which I won 25-24."

In singles game, anything can happen. Bill Boettger also talked about a singles game that he could never forget. "It was the final of the Hong Kong Classic in 1992. Cecil Bransky of Israel was leading Graham Robertson of Scotland by 24 to 4. The game went on for another fifteen ends and Robertson won 25 to 24."

Bill smilingly added, "Isn't that incredible? Never give up in any situation."

Keith Roney, who has been in the National Team since 1988, gets a lot of chances to bowl against top bowlers. "No matter who you bowl against, you have to play steady and consistent bowls with confidence," he said. "I enjoy playing singles against top bowlers such as Jeremy Henry from Ireland, Russell Meyer from New Zealand and Frank Souza from the USA. They don't intimidate me though, because I know my ability."

Alan Webster's memorable singles game for sure is the final game he played against the bowler from Papua New Guinea in the 1999 Asia Pacific Games, when he won the gold medal.

"The secret of winning singles is to focus and also to make the comeback," he reminisced. "I remember when I played the final game in Kuala Lumpur, I made a comeback from losing 7:18 to winning the game after six ends. At the time when I was losing 7:18, it seemed that I would surely lose the game. In my mind, I thought to myself, 'Silver is not so bad. But I better make it respectable – just at least get a double digit.' Then in that end, I won a double, making the score 9:18. Then I played a long jack. After I released the first bowl, I told myself, 'This bowl will be on the jack.' My instinct was right. That bowl was a toucher. I said to myself, 'I can do it anytime.' In that end, believe it or not, I got four touchers. This drove my opponent nuts. He started firing and missed. Since that end, I kept on scoring till I won the game."

This was surely a real comeback and brought the greatest victory Alan Webster ever made in the international scene.

Sheila Buttar's story is on a different note. The most memorable singles game for her was in 1996 when she bowled in the Canadian Championship. "Although the opponent bowled well, yet I just bowled like magic and without any mistake for every shot," Sheila said. "I won the game 25 to nil. The whole game seemed unreal and it was the best game I had ever played."

"The most memorable singles game was the game I played against David Gourlay, who is the world number one player in the PBA." Christie Grahame said.

How good was he? "David was always close. He was very professional and won the first set easily. I regained my composure in the second set and led 4-0. David responded with a two and then three point end to go up 5-4. I responded with a double, moving one shot ahead going into the last end. But it was the measure for the shot of a quarter of an inch that gave David a double to win the game."

After the game, David Gourlay said in an interview, "I was well in control but Christie changed the jack length in the second and I struggled a bit and suddenly he was back in the match.

This new format can alter things so quickly and matches can turn against you in a few ends."

The new format mentioned by Gourlay is an attempt to make the indoor game friendlier for TV. Matches are played over two sets of seven ends, with nine ends for the semi-finals and finals. A one end match tiebreaker is used to decide the winner if players end up splitting the sets.

A one end play-off is also used to resolve tied sets.

There are no "dead" ends. If the jack is shot out of bounds, it is re-spotted at a point halfway between the side of the rink from where it left the green and the "T", which is situated three metres from the ditch, and the end resumes.

In the future, if singles games are going to adopt some new formats, we will have to adjust to new strategies and tactics. It would be a different game to play. Singles is always a challenge to a true sportsperson.

Tips for Playing Singles

by Sheila Buttar

1. Most important skill - first bowl on the jack.

2. Never give up.

3. Singles is a mindgame - your strength and your opponent's weakness.

4. Be Confident – I WILL do it not I will TRY to do it.

5. Singles improves concentration - watch every bowl go up.

6. Take note of the make and size of opponent's bowl to help with your line.

7. Keep the jack – control!

8. Don't let an opponent distract you with conversation - just don't answer and he/she will get the idea.

9. If the opponent favours one side every end - block it.

10. Make use of your marker regarding the position of bowls, not just shot bowl.

11. You determine the pace of game if possible - if pace is too fast, take a walk to the head to slow things down. Don't pick up your bowl until ready to deliver it.

12. If considering changing hand - do it with 3rd bowl not 4th.

13. Walk up to the head before delivery 4th bowl - thus no surprises.

14. Take a walk to the head to calm down or get it together.

15. Use bowls in the head to determine draw weight.

16. Weigh shots - 1 to 2 yards only unless it is a take out or burning the end.

17. For position bowls - make a SPECIFIC spot or bowl as your jack - not just anywhere close.

18. Getting second shot is sometimes as important as shot.

19. Take advantage of any opportunity that presents itself - develop the "killer instinct."

20. Enjoy the game.

More on Tips for Playing Singles

(compiled by Bill Boettger from Jimmy Davidson of England, in Bowls International Magazine)

1. SHOT THEN POSITION: It's always the best first singles priority to draw shot before you even start thinking about position.

2. FIRST BOWLS: Isn't it silly that most bowlers concentrate more on the last bowl of an end than they do on the first. If you apply the same concentration on the first bowl as the last, you are unlikely to be in trouble by your fourth bowl. Be first in the head.

3. SECOND SHOT: It's even more important to get two bowls in the head in singles than it is in other games. The lesser number of bowls means that you are more likely to leave your opponent the chance of a "take-out" with that single bowl in the head. It would far sooner be vulnerable to a trail of a smaller jack than the takeout of a bigger bowl when thinking of position in singles.

4. FAST GREENS/SLOW GREENS: The faster the green, the less you should play shots with controlled weight. On the very fast New Zealand greens the game is drive or draw. If the green is slow, the controlled weight shot has more chance of success.

5. BLOCKERS: Blockers and singles rarely go together. With so few bowls and so many spaces, blockers are usually wasted. The exception is protecting a game-winning lie.

6. THE HEAD-OPENER: The third bowl of an end is the one to use to make room for that last bowl.

7. IN THE LEAD. If you're in front play conservatively to protect against giving your opponent a chance for a big end. The scoreboard in your favour may be the final deciding factor for a safer draw rather than a risky conversion shot.

8. LAST END: Always try to score the last end!

Chapter 6

You Are Not Alone - Team Playing

Ω

SINGLES BRING LAUREL and glory to the individual. And yet a lot of people enjoy team playing more as it involves the effort of more than one person. The interaction of co-operation among team members makes the game more interesting. The more people involved, the more tactics you have to apply. Fours is the most interesting game because every position has a special role to play. When four people are playing together, the combination of team work usually brings out unexpected results. In my personal experience, I won most of my important games in fours.

My Experience

The very first experience in my bowling career was way back in 1989 in Hong Kong. I was only a second-year bowler. Together with three other sophomores from my club, we decided to venture to play in the Colony Fours Tournament, which was supposed to be very competitive. I was pushed to play skip. Being new in the game, the word "fear" was not in my vocabulary. So I skipped the team without any pressure at all.

The games were held in separate weekends on a straight knockout basis. Maybe it was the beginner's luck, but we kept on winning by beating all those more experienced bowlers until we came to the final. My club was excited that we could go that far and a lot of members went to watch the game and support us. As this was a major tournament, even the reporter from the English newspaper went to cover the event. And our opponent, the defending champion, was a strong team made up of Hong Kong Team members.

I remember it was a warm sunny Saturday afternoon. We played on a neutral green. It was indeed neutral to me because I had never bowled on this green before. It was very tricky. At that time, I knew nothing about tricky greens. The only thing I knew was that no matter how hard I tried, my bowls just couldn't get near the jack. I was not the only one. All four of us struggled. It was not a good game to watch. At the 10th end, we were down 1:15. Some of our supporters were disappointed and left. I started to feel sorry for myself. The only thing in my mind was to get a few more points to make the score board look better. Then we scored three, but our opponent immediately scored four. But since that four enders, we kept on scoring until we got double digits. Coming to the last end, we were still down five points. Thinking I could finally come to the end of my shameful performance, I felt relieved and was ready to throw my last bowl. As my hands were sweating because of the heat, I wiped my hands and then rolled my bowl. To my embarrassment, I threw a wrong bias. I lowered my head, assuming my opposing skip would sneer at me. She immediately threw her last bowl. Strangely enough, it followed the line of my wrong bias bowl and ran out of the boundary. Something unexpected happened. As all the bowls were spreading far from the head, and after a lot of measuring, it turned out we held five shots. We earned an extra end. Then in this crucial moment, Grace Chu, my vice, trailed the jack to the back and the opposing team failed to beat it. We won the game!

Nobody in the whole wide world could expect such an outcome. We made the headline of the sports column in the newspaper the following day. Our club was overwhelmed with joy. We held a big celebration party and our picture was hung on the wall of the corridor at the entrance of the clubhouse.

After all these years, I can still remember the important things I learnt from that unexpected victory. The first precious lesson is: never give up even though you are way down. This helped me a lot in my later bowling career, I would fight to the very last minute of the game and never feel discouraged by the score on the board.

The second thing is: it is more fun to win with a team. Yes, you are not alone. When you win the singles, you are the only hero. People may become jealous of you. With a team, you get all the support you need. I can still remember how the four of us with our husbands marched to every game and had great fun together. When you smile, the whole world smiles with you. When you cry, with a team, you are not alone. They are there to cry with you too.

Ideal Team of Fours

Christie Gahame also prefers team playing rather than singles because he enjoys bowling with other people. He likes to bowl with people who enjoy the game. He said, "You have to pick up people you are happy to bowl with. As a team, you have to work happily together. Everyone plays his position and specializes at that position."

Steve Forrest also likes team playing. "Because it is more fun," Steve said. "You can talk to someone before, during and after the game. I would bowl with enthusiastic people with good technical skills, people you can bowl happily together with. Of course, it is good that we can have chemistry. Sometimes it works, sometimes it doesn't."

What is the role of each position?

Sheila Buttar says it is good to have a team in which everyone is carrying out the role of a particular position. Once in the States, she had the good fortune to line up with an ideal team.

The lead would put one on the jack and one behind the jack. She was so serious to be a good lead that she even kept a record of all her shots in every game. The second was the ideal number two. She was the so-called "country bowler" who could put the bowl in any position you ask her to do. The vice could play up shots and prepared the way for the skip.

When talking about the fours team, Graham Jarvis says that the lead's job is simple. What is required of the lead is the ability to play to the jack - no need to be too skillful, The second must have the ability to draw as well as put position bowls. The vice has to help the skip in various ways.

How about the skip? "When you speak about a skip, you must talk about a team," said Graham. "A skip is a team member only. Four skips wouldn't make a good team because each of them only thinks as a skip. They should play according to their positions. In a fours game, the most important thing is to put position bowls. In playing singles, you might play spectacular shots. But it is not so in team playing. It's not necessary to play those spectacular shots. If you are down, put one in the head. Guard against losing a big ender. Don't take risk unless necessary."

Beryl Harrington is also a strong believer in not just putting any four people together to form a team. They must be happy and enjoy bowling with each other. They have to be compatible. "I was brought up in England and had a different concept of team position," she said. "In the team, everybody makes suggestions. Skip is not considered the most important person. There are times when, after discussion, they may make the weakest person the skip when the opponent's front end is strong. No one is upset if they change position."

"Compatibility is paramount!" Bill Boettger said. "Each player must be committed to his or her position and know exactly what their job is." Bill prefers pairs or fours to singles because he likes sharing success and failure. In fact, he did well in team playing in international games. He won the gold medal in Pairs with Ron Jones (the first Canadian international gold medal) and also the Men's Fours gold medal in the 1991 Pacific Rim Games in Hong Kong. Then he won the Men's Pairs gold with Mark Gilliland and the Men's Fours bronze in the 1993 Pacific Games in Victoria, BC. "The lead must be a skillful draw player." Bill Boettger analyses the fours team. "The second should be a variety shot player. A draw bowler if the lead is nowhere or a driver if the opposition has a tight lay. The third must be an immaculate draw player to get the shot or at worst second if the front end has a bad end. The third should also be able to play the weighted bowl to make room for the skip. The third must be on the same page as the skip with regards to shot selection and strategy."

"The skip must be the best all-round player and the one who performs well under pressure. He must draw the shot to save, must draw to add to a count, must be able to drive to kill, must be positive to his or her team at all times. He has the ultimate responsibility for reading the green, deciding the length, and reading the opposition."

Dorothy Macey elaborates more on the combination of an ideal fours team, "The lead has to be able to throw the exact jack and be able to draw. She must be a good draw bowler. The second has to be the strongest player. She can drive as well as draw because she has to break the head up early, loosen up the head before it clusters, while the third has to be a meticulous draw bowler. She must have the ability to draw around front bowls. She also has to have a good sense of strategy. She must have rapport with the skip. She must read the head the same way as the skip does. The skip should know the players. She should be quick to read the green and also quick to put all the information into practice. She must be able to keep the team playing as a unit. She has to have good leadership."

The Key Person

Let's see Alan Webster's viewpoint about a fours team. He said, "The lead is a pure draw bowler. The second has to do everything. He or she must know all kinds of skills, including driving. The third is the next best draw bowler. As for the skip – if the front end has done everything, the skip doesn't have anything to do. All he has to do is to come up and give compliments."

He further explained, "When your front end is doing well, then your opposing skip has to do something. The most he can do is to score only two. If he fails by missing the shot, he may lose six. So if you have the perfect front end, you would eventually win the game. Lead is thc key person. If his first two bowls are always on the jack, then there is a 70% chance you would win the game."

So Alan thinks that the lead is the key person. Doreen Creaney thinks the same. In a team of fours, she thinks that the most important person is the lead. It is not just in theory, because she plays regularly with the same team in which lead Crystal Shepherd consistently draws the bowl to the jack, and they win most games. As for the second, Doreen thinks that a second must be versatile and able to play heavy shots when necessary. The vice must know how to call the head and give the skip the correct information. The skip has to know her players. It is very important for the skip to understand her team members' abilities - the best shot each one is capable of and which can be executed when demanded.

Talking about the key person in the team, Alice Duncalf thinks the second is the most important. "When the lead is not there, you have to depend on the second to be in the head either to do the drawing shot or position bowls," she said, "If the second can't do it, it is more difficult for the vice to do it. When it comes to the vice, sometimes the situation is different. Drawing might be difficult. Then the vice has to throw with weight to get away from trouble. If the vice misses the shot, the pressure will come down to the skip. As a result, very often, the skip may lose big scores by trying to do the pressure shot and failing."

Indeed she is right because Alice won a lot of fours games when Selina Jarvis played second for her. Selina displayed the best skill a perfect second would and she was really the key person in Alice's fours team.

Dave Brown also thinks that number two is the key person because he always played second when he was in the National Team. "When I was in the National Team, I specialized in playing second and won many games," Dave said. "I played so well as a second that I was nicknamed "Dave Cement" by players from other countries. If I couldn't roll my second bowl in the head, the team would be in trouble. It is the second who keeps the team together."

He added, "The skip could be the poorest bowler in the team. He only serves as the motivator. The ideal situation for the fours team is that four good bowlers play together and each specializes in one particular position."

The four scenarios of team work

[1] The best situation

Both you and your partners are playing well and your opponents can't do anything.

[2] The good situation

Both you and your partners are playing well yet your opponents are equally good.

[3] The bad situation

You play well, but your partner is bad.
You have to carry him all the way through.

[4] The worst situation

Your partner plays well, yet you
are struggling all the way.
"Is there a hole where I can hide?"

"Hey, how about both you and your partner are bowling badly, is it a worse situation?"

"No, if both of us are bowling badly, at least I have an excuse for losing a game."

Position

We know that it is important that every team member should be good at his or her position. But how do you fit yourself into a position? Alice recalls that when she was a new bowler, she was keen to go out to play in competitions. But in Stanley Park, all the good and experienced bowlers had already formed their own team and nobody asked her to bowl. So she had to play skip and make up her own team. In the case of Dave Brown, maybe because there were so many good players in England he played lead for 25 years before going into other positions. Beryl Harrington also said that in England, you don't play skip right away. You have to play lead for at least five years. In her club in England, nearly all games were fours. So they learned to play with two bowls only. She remembers that a man in her club used to tell her, "Any fool can bowl with three bowls, a bigger fool can bowl with four, but it takes a 'bowler' with two." He may be right because when you throw more bowls than two, it might not exactly be your skill at work. You might just get the shot by sheer luck.

Beryl said, "In Canada, some new bowlers get to skip too soon. They may think bowling is an easy game. When they go out to play in competitions as skip and get beaten, they might lose the passion. Also, after playing skip, they are not willing to play other positions which might lessen their opportunity to team up with better bowler."

Jim Aitken said that in team playing, he can play lead or skip depending on the situation. "When I started bowling, there were three good bowlers who were my mentors in bowling," he said. They were Jimmy Jarvis, John Henderson and Sam Caffin. These three bowlers said the same thing - every position in a game is important. When I was just a novice, Jimmy Jarvis would sometimes ask me to be the skip and he played lead for me. He would call the shot and usually we won. Now I also do the same thing. I would ask the new bowlers or young people to play skip and I lead and call the head. The young people have the muscle tone which is still there. When people get into the game, they like to skip. We have to show the new bowlers the importance of each position."

"I remember in those days, every Friday, we played 18 end triples and we switched position after six ends. In this way, newer bowlers can learn more about strategy and think independently. When you only play lead, you would rely on other people telling you what to do. To improve your game, you must develop your insight and don't let other people make decisions for you."

No matter how we start, most of us settle down to play in certain positions. Dorothy Macey said, "Some people are meant to play lead. They enjoy leading and are happy to draw with an open jack because they feel less pressure. Actually, a good lead is the most valuable player in the team. So we shouldn't say someone is upgraded to be skip or 'downgraded' to play lead. They are all equal. Some people are more suitable to play skip. Maybe your character helps to decide what you are best suited for. Some people are born leaders and like to take control. They can be developed into a good skip."

That is why Nick Watkins said that you must match your personality with your position. "The lead is usually calm in nature and they are patient to draw and draw to the jack, while the skip is more aggressive. He should be a good leader and earn respect from the team. As a skip, it is not how well you bowl but how well you can direct your team."

Beryl Harrington also said, "In team playing, the skip is the one who is more energetic. You need the personality to keep team members up when down, calm when uptight. You have to keep the certainty. You should treat the team with courtesy and dignity. Don't belittle them. Don't make them feel you're not happy when they throw bad bowls. Keep away from all bad body language."

Trust and Respect

Laila Hassan said, "In team playing, the skip should understand the front end and the front end should trust the skip."

That is exactly what I felt when I won a medal in the second important tournament in my bowling career.

It was in 1999 in Kuala Lumpur when I played the Fours in the Asia Pacific Games. Originally, I was designated to play lead and singles in the 2000 World Bowl in Australia. Because of the withdrawal of Marlene Cleutinx from the team, I was switched to replace her to play as skip in Malaysia because I had been there before in the Commonwealth Games. The committee thought that they needed a bowler who knew the green to lead the three bowlers who were new members of the National Team. Moreover, we are all from BC.

Although I had never bowled with them at home, I knew them by watching or bowling against them. I had some idea of their capabilities. After getting together in the Training Camp, we well prepared for the game. I had a team with people mentally ready for the challenge. Sherrey Sidel is a positive young person with lots of confidence. Sue Smith always puts a lot of effort into doing her best. And Martha Welsh is a person with determination and a fighting spirit.

When we were there in Kuala Lumpur for a week, I had to face the fact that it was not easy for people who were there for the first time to adjust to the hot and humid climate. Also, technically, we were probably not as experienced as bowlers from other countries. Sherrey, the junior singles champion, had been well trained as a good lead, but she had to face all the best draw bowlers from other teams. Sue, the second, is a several-time indoor singles champion and bowls well on fast greens. But the greens in Kuala Lumpur were quite heavy with speeds of 8 to 12 seconds. Martha Welsh, the Provincial singles champion, played as vice but she usually played as skip at home, and her strength is throwing runners. Considering all these factors, I resolved to play aggressive games.

I let my lead to draw close. Whether we were holding shots or not, I asked my second to put bowls in the back. Then the vice could play heavy, either to open the head or trail the jack to the back. If the head was open, I had the confidence to draw to the jack. If she missed, her bowls would be in the back waiting for me to take the jack to the back. This strategy worked well. We won all the games before coming down to the last two teams - New Zealand and Papua New Guinea; the latter like us were also undefeated.

Then we played against the strongest team in our section - New Zealand. Surprisingly, this was the best game we played in the whole tournament. In the first few ends, we played so well that we led 10:0. But they were all top-notch bowlers and caught up pretty soon. When we came to the last end, we were down four points. With my first bowl, I trailed the jack to the back to hold three points. But my last bowl hung out a little bit which was not in the count. If not for that we would have tied the game instead of losing the game by one point. And if we had tied with New Zealand, we would have come out number one in the section and would have been playing for gold in the final. New Zealand tied with Papua New Guinea earlier and we beat Papua New Guinea in our last game.

So we only secured a bronze. But we were so very happy and content to have won the bronze. I bowled the best in my life all because my team respected and trusted me. When I bowled well, I also boosted the spirit of the whole team. It was like a chain reaction in which we bowled well together and really worked as a team.

Teamwork

What is teamwork? It is written in the Malaysia National Coaching Board publication of the 16th Commonwealth Games: "Teamwork is the cooperative or coordinated effort by a group of persons acting together for the purpose of achieving a common interest."

And it was also added in "Our Viewpoint" that "no one can become great by themselves. And no team can become great without the help of everyone, regardless of how much talent one individual may have. In our opinion, teamwork is the single most important aspect to have a successful season."

The Canada's official team logo for the Commonwealth Games is a flying Canada goose.

"because geese are perfect team players. As they fly in a V formation, each bird flaps its wings, creating an uplift for the bird inmediately following."

"A flock can fly about 70% further than if each bird flew on its own. Geese honk from behind to encourage those up front to keep up their speed, and when a goose gets sick or is wounded and falls out, two of its fellows fall out with it to protect it. They stay with the injured bird until it is able to fly or dies."

"That's teamwork and a great reminder that we need each other to get where we are going."

XVI Jeux du Commonwealth Games
KUALALUMPUR

Chapter 7

The Art of Partnership

Ω

THE GREAT RUSSIAN WRITER Leo Tolstoy started the novel "Anna Karenin" by writing "All happy families are alike but an unhappy family is unhappy after its own fashion."

In lawn bowling, the relationship between partners, especially between husband and wife, may be the reverse. Those partners who can't bowl happily together have almost the same stories whereas with teams that bowl happily together, each is happy after its own fashion.

Husband and Wife

Maybe most women whine more than men; here are some of the complaints made by the wives about couples bowling together in a game.

"When we bowl together, he never gives me much information. For example, when I ask him how far my bowl is, he would say, "Never mind about the weight, your green is awful. In daily life, we get along well. But on the green, he gets tense. We never bowl well together."

"When I play badly, although he won't say anything, he shows his discontent all over his face. After losing a game, we would go home without a word about the game. Then we don't speak to each other for three days."

"Even after I drew three good shots in the head, but with only one bowl a yard short, he would pinpoint the blame on me with that short bowl for putting a blocker. He is always negative about my bowling."

"My husband always expects too much from me. Even though I am a National champion, I have my bad days. Once when he started criticizing me, I simply told him, 'You skip next time."

So much is enough for complaints.

"There are a lot of couples who don't bowl well together," John Aveline said. "I remember in Ontario in my club, there was a lady bowler who always yelled at her husband on the green and would be in a rage if her husband made a bad shot. I get along very well with my wife Cathie when bowling together. We never argue. Back in Ontario, we were once flattered by another bowler who was amazed that we never fought on the green. 'It's not natural,' he said."

Cathie Cleveland explained, "It is because John taught me how to bowl. I know the way he bowls and his ability to do certain shots. We never have disagreement on how to play because we see the same shot. Even when he doesn't make a shot to my expectation, I never get cross and would say, 'why don't you try it this way' in a nice way."

How about the time when Cathie is not bowling well?

"Cathie always bowls well for me," John immediately answered. "I have no complaints. We understand each other. We are always positive and nice to each other. Cathie plays a sort of subdued game, while I like to chatter more. We are a good combination."

He continued to talk more about their partnership, "It is interesting how we sometimes switch positions in a mixed event. When we first started bowling together in Ontario, I would play lead and call the shots. In this way, we often put the opponents off. As I am a young bowler, I would intimidate those old ladies who used to lead while Cathie played against the men skips who were uncomfortable playing against women. Now we sometimes play like this as one of our tactics."

The mixed games
Can you guess their relationship?

They must be lovers.

Obviously, they are husband and wife [probably married over ten years].

They are probably a made-up team and they hardly know each other.

Another couple who bowl happily together is Alan Webster and his wife, Robin. Alan recalls an interesting incident where they bowled a mixed pairs tournament in Kelowna.

"It was one of the round robin games. I was lying three shots. I had the last bowl. But I played a bit heavy, moving the jack to the back and went three down. Robin must have thought she was only thinking in her head, but it actually came out from her mouth, 'Alan you fool!' Everyone heard it. The whole green went quiet assuming we would start a row. With a smile on my face, I yelled down back to her, 'Did I do something bad?' Everybody laughed. Oh no, I have no problems bowling with Robin. I always feel relaxed with her."

Martha Welsh and Michael Sanderson are both good bowlers. "A few years ago, we couldn't bowl happily together," Martha said. "We argued, shouted at each other and exchanged unpleasant comments. So we took some time away from each other. Then we worked things out and reached some agreement. At least, we agreed that we should not shout at each other and we should try not to be that demanding. Now we can bowl well together."

Talking about husbands and wives teaming up, Keith Roney said, "When we first started bowling together, Jean tried so hard to play for me and I expected too much from her. Then later, I thought, why should I expect from my wife any differently from what I expect from others? So I changed. Now we bowl well together."

Same thing happened to Ann and Davie Mathie. "Before, we couldn't get along well," said Ann. "When I bowled with Dave, I expected too much from him. I always demanded, 'why don't you do this and that?

More on hushand and wife team

When winning

When losing

But later, I thought to myself: 'I never say such things to my other partners nor do any bad body language to my team. Why do I do it to him?' Now I have changed. We have been able to bowl well for a couple of years now. Now I would say to him on the green, 'If you don't make the shot, no problem, next one.'

"Oh no, we don't say bad things to each other on the green," Jim Dipalo said. "Even if we lost the game, we are still very nice to each other." He smilingly added, "Maybe because we get used to not winning all the time."

But how about the top champion bowlers? Graham Jarvis and Selina were a couple who won nearly all the major mixed events in BC for many years before she passed away.

"The most important thing for a partnership is to avoid disagreement," Graham said. "I never had any problems bowling with Selina. People often said that Selina was lucky to have a bowler like me to bowl with. But I say that I am the one who was lucky to have such a knowledgeable bowler for a partner."

"I remember numerous open pairs events when mixed teams were allowed. Selina would say to me, 'Find a strong male partner to lead for you.' My reply was simple. "You are the best lead I've ever had. You know the game inside out and you use size 6 bowls."

"Of course no one is perfect. There were times when we would both throw bad bowls like everyone else. On one occasion when we crossed the green she said to me, 'Even though you don't say a word I know you are mad by the way you look at me.' When I played the bad bowls and tried to look straight ahead as we passed across the green, Selina would keep walking and softly sing dumb, dumb, dumb, which softened my heart and made me smile."

There are always some little things between a couple which help to make them get along happily together. "In the morning," Graham continued with loving memory, "I would say to Selina, 'Let's try to make this a good day.' At the end of the day, I would say, 'OK, this day is finished, how do you feel?' 'It's a nice day,' she answered."

"When two people live together, you have to work at it - to make things happen or even to make personality change. Try to look for good things. Then you have more to smile on without regret."

Within Family

Husbands and wives have arguments on the green perhaps because of their intimate relationship. They know each other so well that they just say what they think without considering the possibility of hurting the other's feeling. What happens to family members when they bowl together?

Once I bowled against a team made up of the father, mother and their two children. The young daughter was playing lead. When she was ready to throw her first bowl, the mother, who stood right behind her, said, "This is a long jack. Don't be short." The daughter was upset and responded, "Mom, I haven't even rolled my bowl yet. Can you stop nagging me?"

In another game of mixed fours, there was a team of family members. After the game, the mother came to me and said, "I don't know what to do. I'm in the middle. My daughter and her daddy argue all the time."

German Santana and his son Steve can bowl well together. "My son is my best friend," German proudly announced. "We go everywhere together. Steve likes to bowl with younger people rather than adults as they have the same interests and have more fun. But when we bowl together we get along well."

"I bowl well with my brother Adam," Derek Kaufman said. "We know each other well. There's chemistry between the two of us. You can't find two other guys closer than us. We get along fine. We have the same goal and the same attitude."

Ryan Bester and his father won the Pairs in the 2004 National Championship. "We know each other well," Ryan said. "We bowl well together though we don't talk much on the green. When I bowl with my brothers, we talk more - mainly to discuss what shots to play. I have no problem bowling with members of my family."

Bowling Partners

It is a blessing if you can find someone who is a good partner, Most of the time though, we are not that lucky. So what are the things we don't like about our partners?

"The thing I dislike about the team is that their mind is often not on the game. They are not focused. Chatting with other people while standing on the bank is most disturbing. If they try their best, even if they don't bowl well, I wouldn't be upset with them," Martha Welsh said.

"As a lead, I would like to bowl with a skip who is confident and aggressive," Alan Webster said. "As a skip, I need my lead to give me correct information. Don't tell me I am down one when actually I am down four. Also, the lead should not dictate what shots I should make."

Players need to have or develop rapport with their teammates. That's why Sheila Buttar said that partners should have chemistry. "People don't bowl happily together usually because they expect too much from their partners. Nobody tries to throw a bad bowl on purpose. The ideal partner is the one who sees the head as I do, and of course, it is good to bowl with good bowlers."

Marlene Cleutinx mentions that some bowlers keep the same team all the time. Because they know each other well, they often get better results.

"It is a blessing that one can find a compatible team mate." she said. "New bowlers as leads should bowl with different skips to learn more. It is also good for the skips to have different leads.

"I've learned to appreciate different leads. Instead of complaining about your partner, look at her merits, strengths and good points rather than their weaknesses. Just like how you would live with your life partner. A happy marriage is having an understanding of each other. Focus on his good points, then you two can get along well."

Beryl Harrington talked about the three partners she really appreciated. She is thankful that Dorothy Macey had asked her to be her partner in the very beginning. They won gold medals together in the Provincials. When Dorothy talked about Beryl, she said Beryl has sort of a bubbling personality. "Dorothy is more subdued on the green," Beryl said. "I remember there was a game when Dorothy told me beforehand to watch out for the opponents, because they might not behave well on the green. Then I said, 'Why don't we be nice to them to death.' This made a serious person like Dorothy giggle."

"My other partner was Selina Jarvis. I admire her. She was such a lady with lots of inspiration. She brought out the best in me."

A skip has two faces

"Now it is Marlene Cleutinx. We are good friends as well as good bowling partners. I thoroughly enjoy bowling with her."

It is interesting to see how Beryl matches the personality of her partners. Beryl is an extrovert, a cheerful, perky and positive person with lots of confidence. She can get along well with people who are quiet and serious. She and her partner are complementary to each other.

Martha Welsh has found her ideal partner. "I first bowled with Julie Fowler in the National Team qualifier games in Ontario a year ago. Although we had never bowled together before, right from the start, we had an understanding. We thought the same way. I felt so relaxed without any worry. After the game, I told her, 'Without your support and steady determination, we wouldn't have won the game.'"

When the team bowls well together, they have a better chance to win games. Christie Grahame and Jim Logam Sr. have been partners for quite a number of years. They keep winning major pairs tournaments together. Another good pairs team in recent years in BC is the team of Steve Forrest and Hiren Bhartu. Together, they have also won a lot of games.

Hiren got to know Steve in 1995 when he tried to buy new bowls. "He was so kind to sell me a set of bowls - size 7 Taylor Lignoid - by six month's installment. Later, in 1996, he started working for the Children's Hospital in Vancouver. Remembering that I had the required qualification he needed, he offered me a job there and hired me as a casual. We then started bowling together in Pacific Indoor. We work together and we like each other as people. In the beginning, I played lead for him. He taught me a lot of knowledge about bowling. Later, he preferred to lead. Then, in 1998, we switched positions. We won a silver medal in the Provincial Pairs in 200l. Then we won the Fours together in 2002 and 2004."

We can see how good partners affect each other. Hiren becomes a better bowler when bowling with Steve. And Steve, after having withdrawn from lawn bowling for some years, becomes active again in competitive bowling because he has found a good partner.

We are sure happy to see good teams bowling well together in international games and win medals for Canada. Keith Roney bowled with Michel Larue and won a gold medal in Pairs at the 2003 Asia Pacific Games in Brisbane, Australia. The duo went undefeated in the competition.

"We get along well together," Keith said. "We have good communication. We both have the same ideas most of the time."

Then Keith paired up with Ryan Bester to play in the 2004 World Bowl in Scotland, and also won a gold medal. They were described like this in the newsletter, "Roney is known for his solid, consistent and conservative play while Bester has made a name for himself in his brief, but very successful, career by playing an aggressive game and having one of the best drive shots in Canada, if not the world."

"The two are playing really well together," said Margaret Fettes who was at the scene to watch the game. "They are on the same wavelength and that is really helping to give them the success they are producing."

"I get along well with both Michel and Ryan," Keith said. "Both of them play aggressively. I know they can do it and I let them go their way, whether they fire or draw. We discuss the shot sometimes. I give them options and explain the risks involved. Then they play what they feel comfortable with. With my input, they see the risks. There is a good balance between us. They respect my judgment and I trust their capabilities."

I would like to conclude this chapter by quoting Rabbi B.R. Brickner, but allow me to change one word – from "marriage" to "partnership."

"Success in partnership is much more than finding the right person. It is a matter of being the right person."

Chapter 8

In All Weathers

Ω

L AWN BOWLING IS basically an outdoor activity. It is greatly affected by the weather. In Canada, we can only bowl outdoor in the summer season from May to September. In Vancouver, generally speaking, we usually have beautiful, warm and dry weather during these few months. But there are always exceptional days. I remember one year, I bowled in the Provincial Fours game in New Westminster LBC. During the games, there came a hail storm and hailstones the size of small pebbles covered the whole green. We still had to continue to play. It was rather funny to see our bowls jumping up and down on the hailstones.

Weather is always unpredictable in many places. There was a game I bowled in Toronto where we had to stop during a thunderstorm with torrential rain and lightning. People were asked to go inside the clubhouse to avoid being struck by lightning. In my experience bowling in other countries, I encountered all sorts of weather conditions you can imagine. There was torrential rain almost every afternoon in Kuala Lumpur. In Wales, the weather constantly changed from sunny to cloudy, windy to rainy, not only from hour to hour, but sometimes in a matter of minutes.

For a lot of people, any variation in the weather would discourage their performance. For some people, they like the challenge.

The Heat

When the sun is shining, we say it is a nice day for bowling. Alice Duncalf said she liked the heat. "It is a wonderful feeling when the sun pours down on me. The bowl feels better in my hand."

But when it gets really hot, that is a different story.

"I remember once I went to bowl in Papua New Guinea," Dorothy Macey said. "The heat and humidity struck me. I had the feeling of suffocating and couldn't even breathe. The only thing I could do was to shut out all the negative thoughts. I tried not to think about the weather. If you keep on thinking about the weather, you won't be able to concentrate on the game."

"I don't like to bowl in hot weather," Dave Brown said. "This is my weakness. So I try to avoid bowling in hot weather. My strength is to bowl in the morning or in the evening because the green changes quickly. I am quick to adapt to changes. If I have a choice as to the time of the day to bowl, I would choose morning or evening."

It is common sense that on sunny days, we have to put on sunscreen lotion and drink a lot of water.

Jim Aitken had a bad experience of dehydration years ago. "It is no fun to be dehydrated," he said. "During hot weather, we all know that it is important to drink water. I was advised by a specialist the proper way to do it. Not only to drink water, but it is better to drink a water substitute, either juice or pop, in between ends to help retain water inside your body. Drink water even though you don't feel thirsty. Although I don't like the sun much, yet I love when my bowl feels warm in my hand."

The Rain

The most frequent weather change in bowling is the rain. I remember many years ago when I bowled in the Provincial Singles in North Vancouver. It was the day that the Canucks was playing in the Stanley Cup. I was playing the last game of the day. My opponent was a very slow bowler. I was way up in points. Then it started to rain. Every other team had already finished their games and went up to the clubhouse to watch the hockey game. The green was empty except for the three of us: me, my opponent and the marker. The rain was pouring. My opponent was a heavy bowler and tended to be heavy and narrow. After raining, the green changed in her favour. Ultimately, I lost the game. I can still remember that I felt very depressed on my way home after losing that game, and it was a great contrast to the cheering crowd in the street for Canuck's victory. Since that game, I always remember that the green would become heavier and narrower after raining. And I learnt this lesson the hard way.

My other unforgettable bad experience of bowling in the rain was also in the Provincial game. That year, I was playing the Pairs game in Juan de Fuca LBC in Victoria. In the evening, the rain came suddenly and poured. The rain was so heavy and the wind was so strong that my whole body was wet through. I was so cold and wet that I could hardly hold the bowl, but my opponent. Sheila Buttar was well prepared. She had a hand warmer with her and her coat was waterproof. I lost the game, of course. And I actually wanted to give up the game right from the start. Since that game, I always equip myself with good rain gear, a shammy to keep my bowls dry, and the hand warmer always ready in my bowling bag.

Marlene Cleutinx said her way to keep warm in wet and cold weather is to hold a hot water bottle in her hands. "If you cannot keep yourself warm, you can't bowl well with stiff fingers," she said. Alan Webster said, "I hate to bowl in the rain. In the rain, you must have good rain gear and extra grip of the bowl."

Believe it or not, it is lawn bowling:-
after very very heavy pouring rain,
on a bad bad drainage green,
when the green keeper is not there,
and with a bunch of bowlers who are dying
to show their figures!

"The important thing when bowling in the rain is the grip," Steve Forrest also said. "You may have to use smaller bowls - ones you can handle."

Talking about rain, Alice Duncalf said that her worst experience was in Australia. The fast running green of 20 seconds changed tremendously because, all of a sudden, it just rained heavily. She had to find the weight and green again, which were completely different.

"In the rain, you must have the ability to hold the bowl," Graham Jarvis said. "My cradle grip is no problem. If you use finger grip, you may have to change your grip. Another thing is to keep your body dry. I like to hold my umbrella when bowling in the rain."

Wouldn't it be difficult to hold the umbrella and bowl at the same time?

"No. When I am holding the umbrella with my left hand, I would be more careful and sometimes even bowl better. You can pick your line better and even improve your bowling."

Although Graham suggested that I could try to see whether he was right, I haven't had the chance to try it yet.

Laila Hassan has an unforgettable memory of bowling in the rain. It was the Provincial Pairs final game in Ontario at Windsor. Bowlers had to come quite a long way from other places.

"I was leading all the way," she said. "Then the rain poured down when we only had five ends to go. We were four points up at that time. Because of the rain, we had to stop for one hour. When we continued, we were six shots up. The rain came again. Then we stopped for another forty-five minutes. It was getting dark and the green was flooded with water. But we still had to bowl under such condition. My partner could not get up no matter how hard she tried while the opponents were heavy bowlers. We lost seven points and lost the gold medal," Laila sighed. "The weather was not meant for me."

The Wind

Most bowlers from Canada are not accustomed to bowling in strong winds. I had my first experience of that in Cape Town, South Africa. It was really frustrating because the green was keen and the wind was gusty. There were times when I struggled hard with the line and weight. I discovered that in some of the games, I had to adjust to four different weight changes: forehand, backhand, and to and fro from one end to the other end.

Alan Webster had the same experience in Australia. "To play in strong wind is most difficult. I remember the singles game that I played against the top bowler Steve Glasson in Moama in Australia in 2000. It was a 16 second green with a crosswind of 25 knots.

Even Glasson was struggling. When he played the bowls on the down wind side, a gust came up the green, and the bowl was actually carried straight off. When the wind was regular, I used the boundary peck to aim my line. But when the wind was real gusty, I had to aim at the marker on the next green. Finally Glasson won the game 21:16. After the game I asked him, 'Has there ever been a game called off because of the wind?' He said, "If ever, this game was close to being called off. The green was almost unplayable. He won because he had more experience."

Christie Grahame, who also bowled in that tournament, felt the same. "I played the narrow side in such situations. It is not easy. What I do is to forget the last bowl, concentrate on the next shot. You have to remember it is the same to all bowlers."

Bob Scott had the experience of bowling in strong winds in Canada. It was the year that Bob and Dave Duncalf bowled in the Canadian Championship in Montreal.

"There was a thunderstorm attacking the city and a boy was killed by lightning," Bob recalled. "They didn't cancel the game and we had to bowl in very strong wind. Dave was a small short fellow. I still remember the sight of Dave, shakily holding the bowl and his whole body was wavering in the wind like a weeping willow. It looked really funny. Of course we lost the game under such extraordinary condition."

How should we play in windy conditions? Keith Roney, who has a lot of experience bowling in Australia, said, "It is advisable to play into it when the wind is steady and to play against it when the wind is gusty. Because of the wind, the Australians tend to use heavy bowls and they believe bowls without dimples help a bit."

Dave Brown also said that when bowling in winds, it is better to use heavy weight because the bowls would remain more stable in windy conditions. On either hand, they are less likely to be deflected or pushed on by wind and consequently hold their line.

Steve Forrest said he learnt from David Bryant how to bowl in a windy and fast green. "I find this works for me. When the wind is gusty, you play the narrow hand; when the wind is steady, you play the wide hand; when the wind comes from behind, you play forehand; and when the wind comes from in front, you play backhand."

Graham Jarvis thinks that it is always difficult to judge whether it is gusty or not. "My experience is like this," Graham said. "When the wind is blowing from the front or from the back, then try to adjust the weight. When there is crosswind, this is when the line would be different. Some bowlers go with narrow hand. But I think the best way is to go with the wind. That is to let the wind blow and carry the bowl. Play the swinging hand."

Jim Aitken also warned that the wind is never constant. "On fast green, try to have short steps. Do prepare the bowls to take a wide bend. I remember when I bowled in Sydney, the green was 22 seconds. It ran so fast that you had to allow the bowl to go wide and get round in a circle. In such a situation, adjust accordingly - think that if your opponent can do it, you can do it as well."

Maybe this is the right attitude under such condition. Steve Forrest said that when conditions are difficult, just try to be more consistent in the head. Minimize losses, then you can finally gear up. Steve is right to remind us that, after all, this is a mental game.

"When you bowl in different weather conditions or on really difficult greens, ignore the rain, the wind or the bad green. Just do it! Don't give yourself any excuse. The green is narrow? Only 9 seconds or it hangs out? So be it. Never mind, ignore it. Just do it! You are here for the fun! Don't worry, do it!"

Chapter 9

The Lighter Side of Lawn Bowling

Ω

Fun Bowling

L OOKING BACK, I FIND that the first three years were the happiest time in my bowling career and I had lots of fun in club events.

I remember one mid-autumn festival in Hong Kong. The bowlers of our club decided to do something different by hosting a game of bowling in fancy costumes. After a big feast, we put on our different costumes. Most bowlers dressed up beautifully such as in imitation of Cleopatra or an Arabic prince. CP, my husband, picked up an outfit of the devil. When he came out from the changing room, we all couldn't help but laugh. His whole body was covered in a black outfit with two horns sticking out from the head and a curling tail from behind. The funniest thing was that the tights were too tight, showing vividly his whole figure. He was so embarrassed that he had to hold his long curly tail in front for cover, which made him even more funny looking. Of course, he couldn't bowl well on the green because we kept teasing him all the way.

As for me, I dressed up as a chicken with a big head and a protruding beak and my whole body was covered with a yellow robe of feather. On the green, I could hardly lift my head. Whenever I bent down, the beak just dropped down to block my vision. Amid lots of laughter, the game was purely for fun. I didn't win the game but I won "the best costume of the night" and carried home a prize.

The Spider

I asked Alice Duncalf whether she recalls any funny experience on the green. She thought for a while and said, "There was an incident I remember which might seem funny to other people. But for me it was certainly not."

She has a morbid fear of spiders. It was the time when she was bowling in World Bowl in Australia. During the game, she suddenly discovered there was a big spider nestled in her bosom. In great panic, she screamed at the top of her voice and ran straight to the Lady's Room. She took off her shirt and flung the spider to the floor. The spider disappeared in no time. To prove herself a strong woman, she calmly walked to the First Aid Tent to check whether the bite was poisonous. After making sure that she was OK, she went back to the green and finished the game.

"Whenever I remember that hairy spider crawling on my bosom, I still get goose bumps," Alice said with a grimace.

The Toilet

Dorothy Macey recalls the very first time she went to Edmonton and played at the newly built Commonwealth LBC. That was with Selina Jarvis in Pairs for the 1977 Canadian Championship. It was August and yet the weather was so cold that everybody was wrapped up in warm clothing.

There was a game where they bowled on the farthest of the four-green complex. Portable toilets were installed on the side of the green for convenience. During the game, she went into the toilet. But because of the cold weather, the door was stuck with ice and she couldn't come out. In great frustration, she could think of nothing else to do but pound the door and yell for help.

Some men heard the racket and came to the rescue. Don Macey was one of them, not knowing it was his wife. Eventually, the door was pulled open.

"When the door bounced open," Dorothy said, "I must have looked very funny with my thick overcoat and the hood over my head. Red in the face after fighting with the door, I just fell down on the ground. Don must have been surprised to discover it was me in the toilet, and he walked away pretending not to know me. I was quite embarrassed. Then I walked to the green to finish the game trying to forget what had just happened."

The Record

"I don't have any funny stories on the green," replied Alan Webster in his dramatic way of speaking when I asked him to tell me some of his funny experiences. "I only have the saddest story." "This is a story which is not the funniest, but the saddest because I set the record for losing most points in a game. It was in 1968 when I was only thirteen years old and a second-year bowler. I went with my father to watch him play in the four-day-long Seattle Labour Day Tournament. In the Triples game, they were short of a team, so they recruited two second-year bowlers from the club and myself to subscribe as a team and I was placed to play lead."

"I didn't even have my bowls with me. So I borrowed a set from the club. I remember the weather was scorching, but I was sweating not because of the heat. Our very first game was against the current U.S. champions on a 7-seconds green. The first end, we lost seven. The next end we gave up eight. Things definitely went downhill from there. We lost 42:I in ten ends."

"I wonder if I'm still keeping this record of most points lost in a game."

Change Hand

Christine Soukoroff is a left-hander, but she uses her right hand like most people do. At least, she learnt lawn bowling with her right hand.

There was one time when she was a third-year bowler, she bowled with Matt Rogers in a club game. After throwing her first bowl, she was ready to throw her second bowl. Matt, the skip, said to her, "Change your hand!"

Without thinking, she changed to her left hand as told. To everyone's amazement, she rolled the bowl with her left hand and the bowl was right on the jack.

Drive Shot

How forceful can a drive shot be? I have heard the story of a bowler who drove his bowl and hit the concrete bank with such force that the bowl broke in half.

I know a bowler who is famous for firing shots. He likes to bring his new girlfriends to the green and he would point at the hole in the fence behind the green. "That was the hole I made when I fired with my bowl," he says with pride.

I asked Ryan Bester whether he had any funny experience on the green. He recalls once he and his brother were practicing together. For fun, they played different kinds of shots. Then his brother started driving with his bowls. He drove one with great force and hit the bank. Then they saw the bank collapsing in front of their eyes. In the following hours, they were busily repairing the bank hoping the green keeper would not find out about the disaster.

Offending Bowl

Hiren Bhartu hasn't been a long-time bowler, but he learns lawn bowling language quickly. He remembers once when he bowled against Dave Duncalf. Dave pointed at Hiren's bowl and said, "This is the offending bowl."

"What do you mean?"

"I learnt it from bowlers in Australia," replied Dave.

So Hiren said to Dave, "Pardon me, but I hope you don't mind me offending you by giving you a lot of offending bowls."

Dreams Come True

Although Loreen Manns has been a bowler for over 15 years and bowls well, it was only her first time winning golds when she bowled with Helen Lam and me in the Senior Triples of the Provincial Game and the Canadian Championship. It was like a dream come true for her. But she had a differcnt kind of dream come true at this 2004 Senior Canadian Championship in Edmonton. During the whole tournament, she had put her heart and soul into throwing every bowl and gave the support a lead could ever provide the whole team with. She bowled better and better every day and on the fourth day, her bowls were on the jack nearly every end. We won all the way through, beating all the other teams. But on the fifth day, which was the last game of the first round, she suddenly lost her line and weight. A lot of her bowls were either in the ditch or two yards in front. And many times her bowls were wide on the narrow hand and narrow on the wide hand.

After the game, she told me, "You know what, I bowled the whole night in my dream last night and I threw all bad bowls. I can even remember clearly every shot I made. Today is the continuation of my dream. Only it is not a dream, it is real. A bad dream comes true."

I simply told her, "Tomorrow we'll play for gold. Don't dream tonight. You'll be alright."

Next day, in the final game, she bowled really well and we won the game easily. She has made her dream come true. Only this time, it is the dream of being a gold medalist.

The Jack

Graham Jarvis said, "90% of the time, the jack goes back." What happens to the other 10% of the time.

Doreen Creany recalls an experience she had when playing the fours game in the 1997 Canadian Championship in Halifax.

It was a wet day and the game was not going her way. In one end, she was down a number of shots. Then she drove into the head, hoping to move the jack to the back. She was happy to see she made the shot. But to her surprise, the jack spun and bounced up high in the air and then rolled forward. It ended up stopping at about 15 feet in front of the mat. All the front bowls were in the count. She was down six instead of down four.

"I could only console myself with a laugh," Doreen sighed.

Into The Ditch

George Boxwell is a very good bowler. But people remember him more because of his funny stories. Graham Jarvis recalls one about him.

During a BC Final some years ago, with a number of spectators in attendance, George Boxwell attempted to remove Graham's shot bowl from the head by playing a "ditch weight" bowl. The bowl appeared to be right on target as George chased his bowl up the green. However his bowl missed by the narrowest of margins and continued through the head en route to the ditch without touching a thing. George continued to chase the bowl towards the ditch and shouted, "Go in the ditch! Go in the ditch!"

One of two old lady spectators was heard to remark to her friend, "Why did he want the bowl to go in the ditch?"

Short Bowls

Graham has more stories to tell. During a match at the Pacific Games, Graham played against a top Kiwi pairs team, who initially were having a little trouble with the slow greens in Papua New Guinea.

The lead player had played some short bowls during the first couple of ends, and his first three bowls on the third end were still a bit short.

As the lead prepared to deliver his last bowl on the third end, his skip shouted, "Come on up here mate, we've had enough up there!" All in good humour, of course.

Bowl to My Foot

In a pairs match, the lead was a bit inexperienced and was rolling his bowls erratically.

The skip lost his patience, stamped his foot down just behind the jack, and shouted to the lead, "Bowl to my foot."

The lead shouted back, "Heel or toe?"

The Importance of Jack length

Around 1988, an incident was reported in "Bowls International" in Australia. Ian Schuback, the world champion, had started a singles final match with many spectators attending. After a few ends, Ian called on the umpire and requested a replacement jack. The umpire wondered if gamesmanship was involved, and discussed the request with other officials.

Ian had told the umpire that there was "something" wrong with the jack and that the jack might be underweight. The jack was put on a scale and found to be 218g (225g is the minimum legal weight). A replacement jack was provided and the match resumed. This ended the report in the Bowls Magazine.

Around that time, Graham Jarvis had the opportunity to meet with Ian in Vancouver, so Graham asked about how he could hold a jack in hand and tell it was 7g (that is a quarter of an ounce!) under weight.

Ian replied that he just knew there had to be something wrong with the jack because he had selected a spot on the green where the jack should stop. But the jack continued to come up 3 or 4 feet short, and apparently because it was underweight.

Trial Ends

Usually, in trial ends, bowlers try out the speed and line with the jack at the centre. Sometimes people may try out other things. Alan Webster said that he found out something interesting when he played a fours game against the Australians. After the jack was centred, the Aussies threw bowls at different corners of the green instead to the jack. Each bowler seemed to have a mission to accomplish. Maybe in this way, they could get a more complete picture of the green for when there was a need to place a position bowl or when the jack was moved.

"How do you find out the drawing line of the jack at the centre if every one of you does not draw to the jack?" asked Alan.

"It is easy, we just watch you Canadians," answered the Aussie.

Running Across the Green

Most of the bowling clubs in Vancouver are in parks. Surrounded by such natural environments, the greens have occasional visitors from the wood. The most frequent are squirrels and the most unwelcome are skunks. I remember once when I was bowling in Victoria, a dog ran across the green chasing after the jack.

What is the most spectacular scene of something running across the green? Keith Roney said it happened in the 2002 Commonwealth Games in Manchester. When he was playing the Fours game, a woman suddenly took off all her clothes, and carrying a flag ran naked across the green.

"Did she distract your game? Was she caught by the police?" I was curious.

"I don't know what happened to her after. But at that moment, what do you expect we could do? All bowlers on the green stopped and watched her with wide open eyes and smiled."

Measuring

In the 1998 Commonwealth Games, I played the pairs with Marlene Cleutinx. In one of the games, there was a head where Marlene made a beautiful driving shot and moved the jack to the ditch. We definitely had one shot in the ditch and a measure between two more bowls on the green. So we called on the umpire to do the measuring. We watched the umpire, who might have been new to this job, measuring our bowl from the jack. Then, he went to measure the other bowl not from the jack, but from our bowl. He pointed to signal that our bowl had won the measure. Marlene and I looked at each other with amazement. As nobody said anything, we just continued on with the game as though nothing had happened.

Keith Roney recalls another story to do with measuring in the 1993 Pacific Games. There was a game in which he played against the team from Japan. In one of the ends, the Japanese bowler bent down to do the measuring. He moved so carelessly that he not only moved the jack, but practically kicked it far over to the other green. Quickly, he ran to take the jack back and put it at a spot they both agreed upon.

Everything was done in good spirits. Both teams had a good laugh.

In English

In the 1982 Commonwealth Games, Dave Brown played with Dave Duncalf in the Pairs competition. When they played against the team from Papua New Guinea, they saw two black men walking up to meet them.

Dave Duncalf whispered to Dave Brown in a low voice, "These guys are really black, do you think they speak English at all?"

Then they met face to face with these two men and started introducing one another. To their surprise, the opponent skip opened his mouth and spoke in a very English accent, "Jolly nice to meet you old chaps."

The two Daves just couldn't believe it.

"My father is a professor in the English Department of Oxford. That's how I learned my English," the black guy grinned, showing his white teeth.

Wrong Bias

Dave Brown would never forget his first game when he played the Pairs in the 1982 Commonwealth Games. The game was televised live across Australia. He threw his very first bowl and to his embarrassment, it was a wrong bias. The speed of the green was 18 to 19 seconds, so you can imagine where the bowl could land on a fast green with a wrong bias.

In fact, he was not the only one to make the same mistake. On the first day of the tournament, at least 6 or 7 people rolled wrong bias. Apparently it was because the stickers on both sides of the bowls were of the same size. They changed the stickers the next day.

Leg in the Air

Many years ago, Dave Brown bowled in a County Men's Pairs Tournament in England. Their opponents were two old gentlemen, one with a wooden leg. Dave's partner whispered to Dave, "If we can't win this game today, we won't win any game."

But to their embarrassment, they were badly beaten by these two old men. When the game came close to the end, the opponents were holding shots in the head. Dave's partner decided to fire at the head. So he warned these two men to move away from the head. The man with the wooden leg stepped to the side on the bank, and Dave's partner threw his bowl with great force. The force was so great that it hit and bounced sideway, directly at that man's wooden leg. Everything happened swiftly. Swoop. The wooden leg flew into the air and got hung up on a tree top. Then they were stunned to see that poor old man, without uttering a sound, fell flat down on the ground.

"Luckily it's a wooden leg," thought Dave.

Bowling Green

It was way back in the early sixties. Dave Brown and his partner played together in the County Pairs competition. There was a game taking place at a small club called the British Legion Bowling Club in Hampshire.

It was about 30 to 40 miles by car. They drove to the address and, after parking the car, they walked around and couldn't find any bowling green. They saw a man busily walking up and down there. So Dave went up and asked that man where the green was.

"Right where you parked your car," the man answered and then continued his work lining up strings to set up the rinks.

Later Dave found out that it was the way how the local people played lawn bowling - just on a lawn or any empty green space. In those days, it was even legal to play a competition this way.

You Lucky Bowlers

(Written by Stan Corry, Calgary Lawn Bowling Club from Bowls Canada Boulingrin publication "The Green" - Summer 2001)

I have to laugh when I hear bowlers complain about the little trivialities they have to contend with: pay parking at the greens, a one block walk from the parking area, a 40 yard walk to the "far" green, the hedge over-hanging the walking area, no "pushers" readily available. What a spoiled bunch we are when you think of it.

I became a bowler in Northern Ireland in the 60's and that was an education, believe me.

My wife Ray and I both have the experience of being escorted to greens to compete in Cup and League games. The escort was necessary in order that we could get through barriers without harm, these barriers being manned by masked armed men.

The host team's greens were located in a part of the city where British Army helicopters hovered overhead during the games. We never found out if the helicopter crews were bowling enthusiasts or not.

The host team always pulled out the stops for visitors and we were treated very well with a "tea" as it is called there, in actual fact it was usually a full meal following the game. Then the escort arrived to get us out again.

These bowlers were always delighted to see the opposition arriving as there were so many other clubs who wouldn't travel to their green for a game. Bowling always crossed the great division in which we were all forced to live, it didn't matter what you were as long as you were a bowler. I never once heard religion or politics discussed while playing bowls.

I always remember one evening when our club was drawn to play a "country" club in the first round of the Northern Ireland Junior Cup. We were given directions to this venue about 20 miles out of the city.

This was a comparatively new team and a new green set in the middle of a farm. When we arrived, members of the host team were busy removing the droppings left by a herd of cows which had found an open gate and made use of the greens. They then had to fill hoof marks all over the green with sand and rake it over before the game could start.

There is no telling how long the cows had been on the greens but our bowls were reeking after the game. I drove a VW Beetle at that time and the bowls were in the trunk which was in front. The drive home was with open windows. Nothing however that a good wash didn't remove. We won the game and we all enjoyed the hospitality of the host club.

These memories will last forever and I often wonder what the bowlers here in Canada have to complain about!

Bowling Songs

Dave Brown recalls those good old days in England when he had lots of fun in the bowling clubs. The club that he learnt most of his bowling from was called Sphinx LBC. The Sphinx, of course, is the ancient Egyptian lion with the human head, and the club was so called because the director of the company that ran the club owned a car with a sphinx on the hood.

When they had visiting teams, they often entertained them after the games by singing to them over a pint of beer. Here are the lyrics of some of the bowling songs:

Bowling Song No. 1
(To the tune of *Happy Wanderer*)

We are a happy bowling team
We're out to play the game
But if the score says win or lose
It suits us just the same

Refrain

Valeri, Valerah Valeri
Valderah, ha, ha, ha, ha, ha, ha
Valderi, Valderah
My bowls bag on my back

The No. 1 bowls for the jack
They're sometimes miles away
But now and then they strike a patch
And then we cheer their play

Refrain

With shoulders broad the No. 2
Is out to make a play
Wicks off a bowl
And hits the jack
Then gives the shot away

Refrain

At No. 3 the old hands play
To show their skills renown
But if at first they don't succeed
The Skip is still around

Refrain

So now the Skip takes up the stand
We're lying five shots down

But if we have the devil's luck
We may still end one down

Refrain

And now the game draws to an end
And home we make our way
So after giving of our best
A pint to end the day

Refrain

Bowling Song No. 2
(To the tune of the Welsh Hymn *Guide Me Oh thou Great Jehovah*)

When the games of youth have left us
We will to the greens repair
Happy in the joys that await us
In the sunshine fresh and fair

Refrain

Bowling, bowling
Bowling, bowling
Bowling is a bowler's dream
We've been bowling on the green

Now to all you bowlers here assembles

I would have these words to say
Pack your grouses and your grumbles
United in the game we play

Refrain

Bowling Song No. 3
(To the tune of *Lily Marlene*)

Underneath the flag pole
By the bowling green
Stand the greatest sportsmen
The world has ever seen
And there on the green
They draw and fire
With One desire
We all admire
They are the greatest sportsmen
The bowls fraternity

Playing on the fast greens
Bowling in the rain
Friendships last forever
And when we meet again
The times that we had
Will linger on
The memories stay and
Never gone
We are the greatest sportsmen
The bowls fraternity

Bowling Song No. 4
(To the tune of *Forever and Ever Our Hearts Will Be True*)

Forever and ever
Our friends you will be
We thank you for game
And company
There's always a welcome
For you at our greens
When you can join in a game
And then in dream
So may our acquaintance last for ever
We'll play again some summer day
So here's to the next time
We all meet again
And thanks for your jolly good company

"Bowler's Anecdotes"
(From John Aveline's diary)

"I had a game that I was down 9 to 13, then caught up to win by 21 to 13. And today is Friday 13. Am I superstitious?"

"Life is hectic when you have a baby. I was just in time to enter the event five minutes before the game started. With my baby daughter Laurel on my shoulders while skipping, I won the game."

"I got hammered 2 to 41 in twelve ends. (sigh) Not my day!"

"What did I do today? I killed two birds with one stone – striking a jack which went into the next rink and burnt that jack!

"A friend asked me, 'Do you mean Laurel has gone to watch her grandma bowl?' not knowing that it is me and my wife who are the bowlers. (sigh) Lawn bowling is still considered an old man's game in Canada!"

Overheard on the Green

"Oh dear! My bowl is narrow this time!"

"What's wrong?"

"I aimed at the shadow on the green last time and it was exactly the right green. Then I do the same this time, and it is narrow."

"Why?"

"It was the shadow of the tree. I didn't think about that the sun is moving and the shadow keeps shifting."

*

"How good the fourth bowl is when playing triples!"

*

"No wonder it's so dark! How stupid!"

"Why, what happened?"

"When we started to play this evening game, it was still quite sunny. Now the sun has set."

"But on the green the lights have been turned on for quite a while."

"Yes, but you know what? Up until now that I have finished playing the whole game, I discover I forgot to take my sunglasses off!"

*

"I have never bowled such a frustrating game!"

"It's only because you haven't bowled long enough!"

*

"You are short" the skip shouted.

"How short am I?" the lead asked at the other end.

"You should know better than I do. The bowl is nearer you than me!"

More Overheard on the Green

(Collected by George and Carle Pettypiece from Tsawwassen LBC)

"Oh no, not him again."

"I don't know why he asked me which way to go, he does what he wants to do anyway."

"Oh no, another wrong bias!"

"I wish the skips would stop talking and watch what I am doing."

"They should measure that shot."

"Do you think you can come again, the same way?"

"He's late again, ring the bell."

"You know I've never had lessons, I'm a natural."

"Well, we might just as well try and enjoy the game."

"Why is he switching my hand again?"

"I'm being over-coached from the sidelines again."

"I wouldn't have gone that way."

"You would think he would have found the green by now."

"He just left the head, why is he asking me which way to go."

"Oh no, my jack is out of bounds again."

"I wish he would get out of the head and let me make my shot."

"Why didn't he try and block that shot?"

"I wonder if she dyes her hair."

"Stop moving your feet!"

"I don't know why George teaches strategy, he never uses it."

"Why doesn't he go up and look at the head?"

"Please stand behind the jack."

"Women like it really long."

"That bowl is out. What's the matter with them?"

"Foot fault, foot fault, foot fault!"

"How come he never plays that well when he plays with me?"

"He's knocked me up again!"

"That bowl is no good to me out front."

"Why doesn't he move the mat up?"

"You're too tight."

Women's Game Day

This is the day you can see women bowlers coming with their bag carriers.

Women have things of interest other than bowling itself.

The lunch break is a display of home-made food.

"Things of beauty, joy forever."

If that is a moment to be remembered, and someone has a camera.........

Men bowlers also have things of interest other
that bowling itself.

*Even way back in the old times, King Henry VII and
his daughter who later became Queen Elizabath I
often laid a wager on the game of lawn bowling.*

The compliments from female admirers feed their ego.

The Secret

Once there was a bowler who bowled very well. People noticed that every time before he threw his bowl, he would look at a small notebook. After looking at it, he put it back into his pocket and then he threw his bowl. No one knew what was written in the book.

One day he passed away and left everything to his wife. A bowler asked his wife for this book and offered one hundred dollars. His wife gladly gave the book to him. The bowler was so happy, thinking he could get the secrets of how to be a good bowler. He quickly opened it seeking the words of wisdom. To his surprise, the pages were all blank, except for a page in the middle of the book, which said, "Don't forget: small button to the inside."

(Graham Jarvis)

Conceitedness

A well-known lawn bowler was asked to give a talk on his experience of being a champion. In front of a group of enthusiastic listeners, he began his speech by quoting from a letter he had just received.

"You are the greatest bowler in the world," he read. "You are better than David Bryant, Tony Allcock or David Gourlay. And not only are you the greatest bowler, you are also the wisest and most handsome."

For a moment, the audiences were stunned at such an exhibition of conceit. Then the bowler continued with a smirk.

"Incidentally," he said, "the letter is signed 'mother.'"

In Heaven

A bowler died and went to heaven. He told the angel on duty that he was a bowler.

"We have a lot of bowlers here," the angel said.

"Can you show me the bowling green?"

"Sure," the angel answered.

Then the angel led him to the green. There were many bowlers on the green. He saw some bowlers wearing T-shirts with the letters HH on them.

"What does HH mean?" asked the bowler.

"It means Heaven Hotshot," answered the angel.

Then he saw an old man with grey hair and a long beard. He was wearing a shirt with the letters TW on it.

"Who is this old man?"

"Don't you know Him, the angel whispered. "He is God Himself."

"What does TW mean?" he asked curiously.

With a smile, the angel answered, "He thinks He is Ted Waterston."

(Bert Wilson)

In Heaven II

Three bowlers, A, B and C, died and went to heaven. They told the angel on duty that they were bowlers and would like to play In the League.

"No problem, you can join the League," the angel said. "But there is a rule here. There are a lot of ducks walking around at the banks of the greens. You must be very careful not to step on them. If you do, you'll be punished."

So they played in the League and bowled with different bowlers. The angel was right. There were ducks all around the place. They tried to be very careful not to hurt them. But one day, Bowler A carelessly stepped on a duck. The angel appeared and said, "You have stepped on a duck and broke the rule." The angel then brought a bowler who was a very poor player to Bowler A and said, "In order to punish you, you will have to be his partner for the rest of your bowling career here."

On the next day, Bowler B made the same mistake by stepping on a duck. The angel appeared again and said to Bowler B, "You have stepped on a duck and broke the rule." Then the angel brought an even worse player to Bowler B and said, "In order to punish you, you have to be his partner for the rest of your bowling career here."

So Bowler C became very careful in walking around the green. For three months, he never stepped on any duck. Then one day, the angel appeared and brought him a champion bowler, who was actually Bowler C's lawn bowling idol while he was alive. Bowler C was so happy and thought, "This must be the reward for not stepping on any duck for such a long period of time, and now I can have a champion bowler as my partner."

Then he heard the angel said to that champion bowler, "You have stepped on a duck and broke the rule. In order to punish you, you have to be his partner for the rest of your bowling career here."

Chapter 10

The Essence of Winning

Ω

THE FUN OF LAWN BOWLING is not just the physical exercise. It is the game, it is the competition and it is the winning. Winning a game in lawn bowling is the combination of four elements: skill, experience, form and luck.

Among these four elements, most bowlers consider that skill takes precedence over the others, and then maybe experience comes next. In order to play well, we also must be in good form - physically healthy and mentally prepared for the game. And yet, we often hear people mention "luck" in winning or losing a game. People even say that the three L's in lawn bowling are "Line, Length and Luck."

Alice Duncalf thinks that luck is definitely a part of the game. So does Alan Webster who also believes in luck.

"Fluke and luck are the same," he said. "The better the green, the faster the speed, the less luck is a factor. To determine the outcome, skill counts. Skill comes first."

Christie Grahame also thinks skill comes first. He said, "You have to be good to be lucky. There's a difference between fluke and luck."

Graham Jarvis thinks that when we say a shot is lucky, usually we mean it is an unusual wick. "A skillful bowler would make use of other bowls to wick in for the shot," he said. "Some people deliberately make use of bowls in this way, to which then people may say, 'You're lucky.' So the more you practice, the more you have luck."

"Luck is a fortunate break," Steve Forrest said. "The team with more bowls in the head has more luck. But there are times when you should win but don't."

In lawn bowling,
Winning a game is the combination of
    Skill,
    Experience,
    Form and
    ≈Luck≈ !!

Lucky bracelet, lucky scarf or lucky underpants!

"I believe in luck," Martha Welsh said. "Luck follows the brave. There's always luck in the game. You have to be daring to take the chance and you may have a big win in one end when you are lucky. But still skill should come first."

A marathon runner, Margaret Groos said, "When I was 15, I had lucky underwear. When that failed, I had a lucky number, even lucky race days. After 15 years, I've found the secret to success is simple. It's hard work."

Young people such as Derek Kaufman don't believe in luck. "You create your own luck," he said. "Think positively and play positively, then luck will come."

It is good to see young people believe in themselves and create their own destiny. When we get older, we tend to believe in fate. Sometimes, no matter how hard we try, things just don't come our way. To be the winner of a tournament, there is more than the game itself. Sometimes, it is the luck of draw, the luck of timing - different time of the day or the luck of the green.

"Luck" is something we have no control over. With skill and experience, we can only try our best to bowl well. But very often, we bowl well one day and yet badly on another. Why can't we keep our consistency?

"It is because no two games are the same," Laila Hassan said. "No two greens are the same. Every time you bowl on different greens and against different opponents. Also, there's no two heads alike. Every situation is different. All these affect your performance."

Christie Grahame considers that we do not bowl consistently all because of the green. "It is difficult to be consistent in Canada," he said. "The greens are not the same. Every rink runs differently. For example, when I played the Provincial

Singles this year, there was a game I bowled on an end green. My bowling just couldn't cope with the tricky green which was accountable for me losing that game."

Bill Boettger thinks the same. He said, "I've lost too many singles games by me not finding the green and unable to reverse a negative situation. There are too many outside factors such as weather or poor rinks that can influence the outcome of a singles game."

I also have a lot of unpleasant experiences in bowling badly on bad greens. I can still remember the feeling of struggling to throw a bowl on very soft turf. The bowl seemed to sink to the ground and could never get up to the head. For some time, I became haunted by the thought that I was tense when bowling on such green and became mentally defeated. Yes, lawn bowling is a mental game.

A champion bowler may be defeated by a little old lady from a social club. A novice may beat a veteran bowler. The competitive bowler is often obsessed with the thought to strive for excellence and forgets to get a balance. "Trying too hard" may spoil our bowling. It is all mental.

There are also times we bowl extremely well. Is it because of the green, or our form, or something else? Maybe it is in the inner self. I believe there is some hidden power within every one of us. How to release it? It is always a mystery to me. We can never explain how it comes and how it goes. I have been bowling for 17 years and I believe I have acquired a certain standard of skill and experience. But most of the time, I have to work hard to bowl well by reading the green, keeping a consistent delivery and concentrating to carry out the skills, Don't you have the experience of bowling like magic occasionally and can't explain why? I remember two occasions vividly.

On one occasion, it was just an ordinary Tuesday evening when I bowled in a game of Classic Pairs in Vancouver South LBC. There was nothing unusual about the green or the weather. And yet, suddenly I felt different. Everything became so easy. When I threw the bowl, it just rolled so easily out from my hand and went to wherever I wished. There was no effort for me to make the shot I desired whether it was the draw, the take-out or wick-in. My opponents were bowling quite well and in fact my lead was out-bowled by the opponent. When I stepped on the mat knowing I was down in the head, I felt happy because it was so easy to turn the head in my favour. I never missed any shot and won by big scores. But the next day, when I woke up, everything went back to normal. The Superman turned back into an ordinary folk again.

Another incident was when I played the Provincial Singles at North Vancouver LBC about ten years ago. I was the winner of the B Division and played against the winner of the A who was Sheila Buttar. I clearly remember right from the start when I stepped on the mat, I suddenly had a mysterious feeling that I would win the game. The bowls would go wherever I liked. It was just like magic. I easily won the game. In the afternoon, I had to play against Sheila again in the final. But the magic disappeared. I became the ordinary me and lost the game.

How can you explain this phenomenon? We will never know why. Every human being is a wondrous creation of God and there is a lot of mystic power inside for us to discover.

There are bowlers who always bowl like magic. The best performance I have ever seen was a game of V&D Men's Pairs played by Ted Waterston and Bruce Matheson in West Vancouver LBC. Both of them could handle every shot accurately. No matter how close the opposing bowls were, they just got closer. They could easily draw to the jack, tuck it to a better position, place the bowl a few inches behind or trail the jack to the ditch. Both of them played with the same smooth and gracious style. I could see that they thoroughly enjoyed the game, not because of the big scores, but the bowling itself.

Not only top bowlers are able to enjoy the game by bowling well. Every time, when we greet our opponents on the green at the start of the games, we say to each other, "good bowling." It is not just the winning, it is the "good bowling" which is the true meaning of playing. We all take personal pride from "making the shot,". however fleeting that moment may be.

I remember in the 2004 Royal City Tournament in New Westminster LBC, my husband CP partnered with Clement Law. There was a game they played against the Kaufman brothers. It was on an end green, but the green ran well. I sat on the bench to watch - enjoying all the good shots they made. Later, I left to run errands. When I came back, they had already finished the game. CP was chatting with Clement with a smile on his face. "They must have won the game, judging from the way they look," I thought to myself.

"We lost," CP told me, "but we enjoyed the game very much. The four of us bowled really well. I made the shots I wanted and it was a good game."

I always remember what a bowler told me when I bowled in the Atlantic Rim Games in Cape Town. We got to know some of the local bowlers when we practiced before the Tournament. When I finished a game of Singles, one of them came up to me showing his appreciation of my bowling. Then he said to me, "I am sure in the future, you'll win more than you lose." I considered that a great compliment.

When we are new bowlers, we only think of winning every game and consider losing a game a shame. The longer we bowl, the more we understand that nobody can win every game. There is only one winner in each tournament. If you can win two or three out of ten, you should be happy, not to mention five out of ten. If you can win more than you lose, you must be a very good bowler.

Life is a journey of discovery of what one can do and we are lucky to find a sport that we really enjoy. The fun is not only winning. Self-esteem does not come from winning, but from admiring ourselves for what we can do. The fun of bowling is to bowl well and to achieve what you want to achieve. Winning is the bonus.

In this book, we are fortunate to have so many good bowlers who are kind enough to share their experiences with us. Like digging for treasures, we have the gem at the very end of the treasure hunt. If this book really interests you to read up to this page, you've got this best piece of advice. This is the "Da Di Da" list I mentioned earlier, provided by Graham Jarvis, the precious wisdom accumulated over 60 years of bowling.

Good luck, great bowling and enjoy your game.

The "Da Di Da" List

1. Most bad shots are played because the player concerned has lost concentration.

2. Minimize the use of a bad hand.

3. One bad bowl can cost you the end. One bad end can cost you the match.

4. Many a game has been lost through poor bowling of the jack.

5. Tired players play tired bowls. You must be physically fit and mentally alert.

6. 90% of the time, the jack goes back.

7. Short bowls are generally of little value.

8. Never change a winning length.

9. 90% of the time, the result of the end is dictated by the action of the last 3 bowls.

10. Never be in a hurry to play a bad bowl. Rushing the delivery will produce inconsistency.

11. The art of being a good tactician is to contain the opposition to a minimum of shots.

12. A good skip should be an aggressive thinker.

13. The running shot is one played with at least ditch weight; i.e., if you miss your object you will lose your bowl. It is important to remember that more grass is required on a heavy green than a fast green for a running shot.

14. If you get complacent, you set yourself up for failure.

True champions
are like a tea bag –
They become strong
in hot water.

"He ain't heavy, he's my brother."

Bowler's Prayer

By Carol A. Harradine

(From "The Green" - summer 2004)

Bowling's my pleasure; I shall not want.

It maketh me to walk and down green pastures,

And leadeth me to compete in competitions.

It restoreth my gamesmanship

And leads me in the path of David Bryant for the game's sake.

Yea, though I bowl in the wind and rain,

I will fear no evil.

For my skip is with me.

My measure and chalk, they comfort me.

Thou preparest a rink for me

In the presence of mine opponents.

I anointest my bowls with Grippo

And my bowls runneth true,

Surely good wicks and lucky shots

Shall follow me all the days of my life

And I shall dwell on my Bowling Green forever.

Profile of the author:
On-Kow Au

Education: B.A. University of Hong Kong
Profession: Radio Broadcaster, Writer

Bowling career:
1987 Started bowling at Craigengower Cricket Club in
Hong Kong
1989 Immigrated to Canada
1997 – 2000
5 times Provincial Champion
Twice National Champion
1995 – 2000
Canadian National Team member

International appearances:
1997 Atlantic Rim Games
Singles & Triples (lead)
1998 Commonwealth Games
Pairs (lead)
1999 Atlantic Rim Games
Singles & Triples (lead)
1999 Asia Pacific Games
Triples (skip) & Fours (skip) Bronze medal

Service
2003 – 2006
Director of Athletic Development Program,
Bowls BC, Canada

ℬ𝒞 ℒawn ℬowling 𝒞lubs Directory

Vancouver and District

1. Burnaby North LBC
Confederation Park, Willingdon & Penzance, Burnaby
Tel. 604-298-5817

2. Coquitlam LBC
640 Poirier Street, Coquitlam Tel. 604-939-9808

3. Dunbar LBC
3850 W. 31st Ave at Highbury, Vancouver Tel. 604-228-8428

4. Granville Park LBC
3025 Fir Street (at 14th Ave) Vancouver Tel. 604-731-8422

5. Kennedy Park LBC
11760 88th Ave, Delta Tel. 604-583-3793

6. Kerrisdale LBC
5870 Elm Street, Vancouver Tel. 604-261-1116

7. Ladner LBC
5128 42nd Ave. Ladner Tel. 604-946-6722

8. Langley LBC
20471 54th Ave, Langley Tel. 604-514-2695

9. Mann Park LBC
14560 North Bluff, White Rock Tel. 604-531-0833

10. Maple Ridge LBC
11445 232nd Street, Maple Ridge Tel. 604-167-0755

11. New Westminster LBC
710 8th Street, New Westminster Tel. 604-524-5623

12. North Vancouver LBC
2160 Lonsdale Ave., North Vancouver Tel. 604-985-2321

13. Pacific Indoor LBC
Millennium Sports Centre (near Queen Elizabeth Park)
Vancouver

14. Richmond LBC
7321 Westminster Hwy, Minoru Park, Richmond Tel. 604-276-2695

15. South Burnaby LBC
4000 Kingsway, Central Park, Burnaby Tel. 604-437-3545

16. Stanley Park LBC
2099 Beach Ave. Vancouver Tel. 604-683-0910

17. Surrey LBC
18513 70th Ave., Clayton Park, Surrey

18. Tsawwassen LBC
331-1050 54A Street, Delta, Tel. 604-943-6882

19. Vancouver LBC
Queen Elizabeth Park, 33rd & Cambie, Vancouver
Tel 604-879-896

20. Vancouver South LBC
4850 St, Catherines St., Vancouver Tel. 604-874-3038

21. West Point Grey LBC
4376 W. 6th Ave. Vancouver Tel. 604-224-6556

22. West Vancouver LBC
650 20th Street, West Vancouver Tel. 604-922-0411

23. White Rock LRC
1079 Dolphin Street (at Pacific), White Rock Tel. 604-536-2616

Mainland Interior

1. Chilliwack LBC
99350 Edward St., Chilliwack

2. Christina Lake LBC
Christina Lake

3. Kamloops Riverside LBC
Riverside Park, Kamloops

4. Kelowna LBC
Corner of Abbot & Leon Ave., Kelowna Tel. 250-762-5911

5. McArthur Park LBC
Kamloops

6. Merrit LBC
2236 Jackson Ave., Merrit

7. Osoyoos LBC
Gyro Beach Park, Osoyoos

8. Penticton Lakeview LBC
260 Brunswick St., Penticton Tel. 250-493-8662

9. Prince George LBC
between Watrous & Wainwright Streets, Prince George

10. Quesnel LBC
600B Johnson Ave., Quesnel

11. Salmon Arm. LBC
691 28th St. N.E., Salmon Arm

12. Vernon LBC
Polson Park, Vernon Tel. 250-542-0212

Vancouver Island – South

1. Burnside LBC
274 Hampton Rd., Victoria Tel. 250-381-5743

2. Canadian Pacific LBC
720 Belleville St., Victoria Tel. 250-385-3577

3. Central Saanich LBC
1800 Hovey Rd., Saanichton Tel. 250-652-4774

4. Cowichan LBC
First St. Centennial Park, Duncan Tel. 250-748-6542

5. Gordon Head LBC
4105 Lambrick Way, Victoria Tel. 250-721-1331

6. Juan de Fuca LBC
1767 Island Highway, Victoria Tel. 250-474-8623

7. Lake Hill LBC
3930 La Salle St., Reynolds Park, Victoria Tel. 250-727-6525

8. Oak Bay LBC
Carnarvon Park, 2190 Harlow Drive, Victoria Tel. 250-592-1823

9. Saanich Indoor LBC
Pearkes Arena, 3100 Tillicum Rd., Victoria

10. Sidney LBC
#4 - 9769 Fifth St., Sidney

11. Victoria LBC
Park Blvd & Cook St., Beacon Hill Park, Victoria Tel. 250-383-5851

12. Victoria West LBC
Victoria West Park (off Esquimalt Road). Victoria Tel. 250-382-0751

Vancouver Island - North, and Powell River

1. Beban Park LBC
2331 Troy Anne Way, Nanaimo

2. Courtenay LBC
Bill Moore Park, 23rd St. and Kilpatrick Tel. 250-338-8221

3.Nanaimo LBC
500 Bowen Rd., Nanaimo Tel. 250-753-7788

4. Parksville LBC
149 Stanford Ave., Parksville Tel. 250-954-3930

5. Port Alberni LBC
4255A Wallace St., Port Alberni Tel 250-724-3354

6. Powell River LBC
5714 Marine Avenue, Powell River Tel. 604-483-9296

7. Qualicum Beach LBC
665 Jones St., Qualicum Beach Tel. 250-752-3459

Made in United States
Orlando, FL
28 June 2024

48373171R00114